# SOCI
## AN ANALYSIS OF ITS PAST AND FUTURE

# SOCIALISM
An Analysis of its Past and Future

by
Erzsébet Szalai

CEU PRESS

Central European University Press
Budapest   New York

©2005 by Erzsébet Szalai
English translation © by Vera Gáthy

*Published in 2005 by*
Central European University Press

*An imprint of the*
Central European University Share Company
Nádor utca 11, H-1051 Budapest, Hungary
Tel: +36-1-327-3138 or 327-3000
*Fax:* +36-1-327-3183
*E-mail:* ceupress@ceu.hu
*Website:* www.ceupress.com

400 West 59th Street, New York NY 10019, USA
*Tel:* +1-212-547-6932
*Fax:* +1-646-557-2416
*E-mail:* mgreenwald@sorosny.org

Translated by Vera Gáthy

While writing the book, the author participated in the research program of the Institute for Political Science of the Hungarian Academy of Sciences.

The translation of this book was supported by the Company Bábolna.

All rights reserved. No part of this publication may be reproduced, stored in a retrieval system, or transmitted, in any form or by any means, without the permission of the Publisher.

ISBN 963 7326 29 4    paperback

Library of Congress Cataloging-in-Publication Data
Szalai, Erzsébet.
  [Első válaszkísérlet]
  Socialism : an analysis of its past and future / Erzsébet Szalai.—1st ed.
    p. cm.
  Includes bibliographical references.
  ISBN 9637326294
  1. Socialism. 2. Socialism—History. I. Title.

HX36.S96 2005
335—dc22
                            2005021620

Printed in Hungary by
Akaprint Kft., Budapest

# Contents

Preface .................................................... 1

CHAPTER 1
The Power Structure and Ownership Relations
of Semiperipheral Socialism .............................. 3

CHAPTER 2
Power and Society ....................................... 13

CHAPTER 3
The Issue of Interest Integration ........................ 25

CHAPTER 4
Actors of the Open Crisis ............................... 37

CHAPTER 5
The Socio-Cultural Heritage and Its Structural Effects .......... 47

CHAPTER 6
The One-Party System and the Transitory Society ............. 53

CHAPTER 7
The Message ............................................ 63

CHAPTER 8
The Chances of the New Socialist Alternative ................ 65

Bibliography ............................................ 75

# Preface

This is not my first attempt at an academic approach to what has been called 'really existing socialism'—or, more briefly, 'existing socialism'—our 'worst recent past.' My present endeavor is directly motivated by the welcome debate that began in the periodical *Eszmélet* (Consciousness); Péter Szigeti's thoughtful paper launching the debate induced me to reconsider and bring together my theses about that system, which disintegrated fifteen years ago. While writing my response (published since) I felt with growing certainty that I would have to expound my thoughts in a longer study, in greater detail and in a more differentiated and complex form. Here is the result of this enterprise.

My work was easy and difficult at the same time, because my basic socialization took place in the system of 'existing socialism,' and the larger part of my life belongs to that historical period. I retain many pleasant memories, but I also had two painful and decisive experiences: my communist father was arrested before my eyes on trumped-up charges in the early 1960s, and subsequently, as a result of my open support for the democratic opposition, I myself had to face the punitive machinery of power in the early 1980s.

Nevertheless, my leftist values, deriving from my childhood socialization and later confirmed by my social experiences, withstood these ordeals and ultimately emerged from them stronger. Primarily I feel that (not least) as a result of my personal traumas I succeeded in breaking away from a very bad leftist tradition of unquestioning trust and fanaticism. Therefore, I hope, my smaller and larger disappointments could not, and still cannot, undermine my basic values.

I have not given this glimpse of my life and my values for their own sake. Although I have always tried and still try to analyze society objectively, I do not believe in a science free of values. In this context it is worth quoting Gunnar Myrdal (1998): "It has been a misguided endeavor in social science for a little more than a century to seek to make 'objective' our main value-loaded concepts by giving them a 'purely scientific' definition, supposedly free from any association with political valuations. To isolate them from such association, new and innocent-looking synonyms were often invented and substituted. On logical grounds, these attempts were doomed to failure. The load of valuations was not there without a purpose and a function, and they soon pierced through the strained 'purely scientific' definitions and even crept back into the specially fabricated synonyms." According to Myrdal, this is the reason why an academic must state his or her values and involvement explicitly, so that the reader may be able to disregard them as far as possible.

From the start, my work claimed to be a leftist critical analysis of 'existing socialism,' and I could rely on predecessors with a similar set of values, including my 'old self.' My advantage over them is that to the chronicler of today the main characteristics of 'existing socialism' become visible in some historical perspective.

It was the economic system of 'existing socialism' that formed the focus of my earlier works on the topic, and today I still see its main features in that way. This piece differs from the earlier ones in three respects. It extends the scope of the analysis to the study and presentation of broader social and socio-psychological processes and mechanisms apart from the economic ones (while insisting on their primacy). It attempts to fit the problem of 'existing socialism' into a "world-system problem." Last but not least the basic conditions of 'existing socialism,' as reflected in the mirror of the new capitalism that has now emerged, seem to be far more complex and today it is not only possible but also indispensable to interpret and assess these conditions in greater detail and from a greater variety of angles.

A major part of this work is taken up by the analysis of those internal and external factors that have led to the fall of the system, and the last substantial chapter outlines the possibility of a 'new socialist' alternative. The reason is that in my view the challenges of world-system dimensions, provoking socialist thoughts, are still valid, and indeed growing in strength.

This study is written in the form of an academic essay. It is academic, because it tries to present its subject in all its interrelationships and complexity. And it is an essay partly because I do not and cannot present the entire literature on the subject, which would fill a library, and partly because I am unable to make myself totally independent of the decisive experiences I have undergone in my own country, Hungary.

Many people were helpful in the discussion of a shorter essay which provided the basis of this book. Above all I wish to mention Iván Berend T., Béla Galló, Gábor Gellért Kis, Tamás Krausz, Tibor Kuczi, Péter Somlai, Péter Szigeti, Róbert Tardos, and Ágnes Utasi. I express my gratitude to them.

September, 2005. *Erzsébet Szalai*

CHAPTER 1

# The Power Structure and Ownership Relations of Semiperipheral Socialism

The leftist critical analysis of 'existing socialism' has produced a significant body of literature. The most relevant approaches from my point of view were made by the theoretical ancestor Trotsky (1976, 1977) and later by Djilas (1957), followed by György Bencze – János Kis (1983), György Konrád – Iván Szelényi (1989) and Ferenc Fehér – Ágnes Heller – György Márkus (1991).

The findings of the Hungarian authors differ at several important points, but they all agree in that they do not regard 'existing socialism' either as a socialist or a capitalist, or even a transitory society: according to their definition it constituted an autonomous social and economic system. (In what follows I will not discuss these authors' concepts in detail, but will express my agreement or disagreement with them as I expound my own position.) My own thesis is that the social formation called state socialism was in reality a social system located between state socialism and state capitalism—a transitory society which it would be more legitimate and exact to call semiperipheral socialism. Therefore my stance is closest to that of Trotsky and Djilas.

My theoretical starting point is that while in a capitalist society based on capitalist private property—where therefore the economy is basically integrated by the market as defined by Károly Polányi (1976)—power relations may be deducted almost directly from ownership relations, while in 'existing socialism,' where (at least originally) the integrating factor was redistribution, the causal relationship is reversed: ownership relations may be deducted from power relations. I am going to follow this logic in my presentation.

## THE HOLDERS OF POWER, ITS SOURCES, AND THE ISSUES OF LEGITIMACY

Who were the holders of power in the system of 'existing socialism'? In fact, what *is* power, and what are its sources? Let us begin with Max Weber's (1967) definition, which is eminently suited to grasping the conditions of 'existing socialism': "In general, we understand by 'power' the chance of a man or a number of men to realize their own will in a social action even against the resistance of others who are participating in the action. 'Economically conditioned' power is not, of course, identical with 'power' as such. *On the contrary, the emergence of economic power may be the consequence of power existing on other grounds.*" (Italics mine, E. Sz.)

The Stalinist phase of state socialism was characterized by the monopoly on power of the *ruling status group*, to use the terminology of György Konrád and Iván Szelényi. Trotsky spoke about a *ruling caste*, meaning the party and state bureaucracy. The power of the ruling status group, or ruling caste, is clearly not based on economic but on political foundations. Its essence is pressure exerted through the power-enforcement machine, affecting even the sphere of private life.

As a result of revolutionary movements sweeping through the Soviet empire, Stalinism had broken down by the late 50s and early 60s, and the post-Stalinist phase of state socialism had begun. Several analyses have been produced comparing the two periods, but they will not be presented here; I will concentrate only on the unchanging and changing elements of the nature of power.

According to Konrád and his colleagues, the stability of the post-Stalinist period was based on the compromise alliance of the ruling status group performing teleological functions—essentially continuing the traditions of the previous period—and the technocracy. Both groups consisted of intellectuals intent on fully developing their comprehensive class rule. While in capitalist societies it is the ownership of capital that legitimizes disposal over surplus production, in state socialism, the "modern system of redistribution," it is the redistributor's or intellectual's knowledge that has the same function of according legitimacy.

Several problems, however, emerge in relation to this extraordinarily clever logic. The most important one derives from the fact that the authors have not consistently considered the consequences of their definition of the intellectual. According to that definition, "it is not knowledge that makes someone an intellectual, but the fact that he has no other entitlement than his knowledge to take up his status." Further: "therefore the intellectuals are the monopolistic owners of such knowledge as is accepted by society as being transcontextual, and therefore used by it to orient its members." And: "Society, or at least the general understanding of intellectuals, qualifies as valuable only those forms of knowledge that have any reference to concepts regulating the spontaneous teleology of society. Such forms of knowledge may at least be related to issues like what is good, what is bad, and what should be done." If the authors quoted had said that a person regarded as an intellectual was legitimized *exclusively* by his specific knowledge as characterized above, I would agree with them. The problem arises from the fact that the position of those in power in the classical phase of the post-Stalinist period was not exclusively legitimized by this specific knowledge, just as it had not been in the Stalinist period. Moreover, the significance of this knowledge was rather modest. Furthermore: *power in the Stalinist period was not at all legitimate, and its legitimacy in the post-Stalinist period was also rather low.* In other words, it was not the intellectuals who were in power (although this does not mean that a group of intellectuals had no share in it). Who then were the real owners of power?

In keeping with, and further developing, the logic of Trotsky, Djilas, and their disciples, it was the party and state bureaucracy—the bureaucracy of the state party and the party state—and the stratum of big-company managers who possessed power. In fact, according to broad empirical evidence, it was these groups who made the fundamental decisions related to redistribution, and who could assert their will against the rest of the society. The power position of big-company managers emerged as a result of the major wave of company mergers in the 60s and of the economic reforms aiming at slow market development, because these processes enhanced the decision-making competency of big-company managers by leaps and bounds (Schweitzer, 1982; Szalai, 1981, 1989; Voszka, 1983; Kornai, 1993).

In the satellite countries of the Soviet empire, the source of power held by those in authority was largely an *external* one. The party and state bureaucracy enjoyed the support of the Soviet party leadership, and the Soviet market offered unlimited opportunities of sales and the acquisition of raw materials for the big companies, that is, for their managers.

The rather low social acceptance of the system, that is, *its legitimacy in the sociological sense of the term*, was maintained by the principle of "who is not against us is with us." One of the major achievements of the revolutionary movements of the 1950s was the continuous satisfaction of individual consumer demand, carried out slowly but on a rising scale, and the lasting 'incorporation' of the related social demand. On the other hand—and this change was most spectacular in Hungary—authority had no further claim on the private lives of the people. According to Júlia Szalai (1988), the families "in their restored freedom" built a work ethic, aims in life, and attitudes that were well-founded in social history, along lines broken off by the war and made impossible by dictatorship up to the mid-1970s. Thus the peasants', clerks', and workers' prewar aspiration to become petit bourgeois could be realized, and that on a very broad societal base despite the political, institutional, economic, occupational, and societal rearrangement that had taken place.

Thus the main source of legitimacy was represented by a continuous improvement of living standards and by the tolerated existence and growing influence of the second society and economy. Since the fabric of societal integration was not institutionalized, the second society and economy were built close to the first, and the relationship between power and the individual was characterized by an attraction to the borderline between the institutional and the noninstitutional, by an informal and individual separate bargain.

The *internal legitimacy of power*—in other words, the arguments by which those in power proved the 'rightfulness' of their power in their bargaining and justified the necessity of enhancing their power or influence—was of greater significance than the low level of societal acceptance of the system. In fact it was this internal legitimacy that guaranteed the internal cohesion of those in power, on the one hand, and the necessary room for maneuver in the struggle between groups with different interests within the organization of power, on the other. (Here I am using the term 'legitimacy' in a somewhat unusual sense, but have not been able to find a better one to describe the phenomenon.)

There are clear differences between the basis, method, and arguments concerning the legitimacy of the ruling estate (the top party leadership), of technocracy (that part of the state party and party state outside the top party leadership), and of the managers of large firms. The internal legitimacy of the ruling status group was based on the fact that it was this group that guaranteed the internal cohesion and mutual loyalty of those in power primarily by asserting party discipline (in which this status group in particular had a primary interest). A 'past in the movement' was a rather weak base of personal legitimacy; the argument that the "Soviet leadership trusts us" was much stronger; and strongest perhaps was the 'negative' argument that in Hungary "we are implementing the maximum of reforms under the given conditions of foreign policy: we are still the best, and only worse people could follow in our place." It is common knowledge, but rather significant that the most important and fundamental arguments of legitimacy were unofficial ones, mostly stated in conversations in corridors: in other words, it may be said with some exaggeration that the internal legitimacy of the ruling status group was primarily a *corridor legitimacy*.

While the basis and arguments of the internal legitimacy of the ruling status group were primarily political, those of the technocracy and large-firm managers were primarily economic. The officials of the functional governing organs of the state bureaucracy, and their associates in the party bureaucracy, pleaded the requirements of the general external and internal balance of the country's economy (and the need to improve it). The officials of the local branches and territorial institutions, and the managers of big companies closely cooperating with them, were responsible for specific areas of the economy: consequently the major means of asserting their internal legitimacy and interest was to prove that their branch, specialization or territory was important and even indispensable for the external and internal balance of the economy as a whole.

At the same time, the officials of the local branches and territorial institutions, and the managers of big companies, in their quest for legitimacy did not avoid political arguments either. In fact, political arguments acquired primacy in certain periods—to mention only the change in the economic policy opposing reform in 1972, when the leaders of branches and the managers of big companies successfully fought for the exemption of the fifty biggest firms from general regulations, by referring primarily to the interests of the workers in big industries (Szalai, 1981).

So far I have discussed the bases and arguments the ruling status group, on the one hand, and the technocracy and the managerial stratum of big companies, on the other, used to legitimize themselves in front of each other. An additional important part of internal legitimacy was the acceptance of, and support for, each group *by* the other (although the level of legitimacy ensured in this way was hardly more than what was called by Csaba Gombár [1983] an "apathetic readiness to follow"). The ruling status group canonized the economic power of the technocracy and of the big-company managers by its own political means, while in return the technocracy and the stratum of big-company managers continuously justified and stabilized the political power of the ruling status group by their economic achievement.

## CLASS OR STATUS GROUP?

Having introduced the concept of economic power one may ask: did those in power in 'existing socialism' constitute a class or were they some other kind of social formation?

In the wording of Marxism, history was nothing but the history of class struggle, while Max Weber uses the concept of class exclusively to describe the structure of market economies, and the category of status group to describe nonmarket, i.e. 'redistributive,' economies. In his view, class positions emerge exclusively through the mediation of the market, and the position of the class in power can be explained exclusively by economic causes. He points out that status groups are primarily *communities* based on a common way of life and a common set of values, but adds: "For all practical purposes, stratification by status goes hand in hand with a monopolization of ideal and material goods or opportunities, in a manner we have come to know as typical." Classes may function as status groups, but they do not necessarily do so.

I have serious reservations concerning Max Weber's, and therefore Károly Polányi's, conceptualization. Although it is true that the proportion of redistributive and market elements is different in each society, a pure redistributive or a pure market economy cannot be envisaged even as an ideal type, because in this respect every society is a 'mixed' one. Therefore 'existing socialism' was also a 'mixed' society. However, this does not mean that we must abandon the use of Max Weber's concepts—or those of Marx either.

The self-regulating market (the mechanism of demand–supply–price) did not operate—or, if it did, played only a weak part—in the economy of 'existing socialism.' Nevertheless, there was a market economy, although in different degrees, in the different countries, one reason being that an increasing number of *market elements* entered the behavior of economic units as the conditions of the period unfolded (Gábor, 1981; Szalai, 1989b).

> "The behavior of economic units shows a market element, or elements, when the economic organization manifests one or part of the following modes of behavior: it flexibly adjusts to conditions of demand and supply; it acts in the same way when it is autonomously interpreting the indirect expectations of the party and state bureaucracy; it strives to assert its own economical considerations in the course of adjustment; in managing the means of production it is guided by considerations of adjustment to market conditions and of economical operation; in shaping its external relations it is guided by similar considerations." (Szalai, 1989b).

The position of those in power is explained partly by political and partly by economic factors. As mentioned before, the ruling status group was originally and basically a political phenomenon. After the Stalinist phase, however, in order to stabilize its power, it was obliged to extend the authority of the technocracy and to create a stratum of big-company managers, who, having been puppets, now came to life. The technocracy and the managers of big companies acquired significant economic power, which primarily meant that they could endanger the stability of the ruling status group by holding back their output. Therefore the relationship between the ruling status group, the technocracy, and the stratum of big-company managers was a dual one: in so far as it was in their common interest to preserve their joint power position they depended on each other, but behind this united front there was an ongoing struggle for the extension of the power of one party to the detriment of another.

It is time, however, to put the question: who constituted the ruling status group, that is, the top party leadership? It was the members of the Political Committee and the party bureaucracy directly serving them. It was they in whom, at least formally, the teleological functions were centralized. The Central Committee was the forum of interest conciliation between the ruling status group, the technocracy, and the managers of big companies, although in a general sense all the institutions of the party and state bureaucracy had the same role. In addition to the conciliation of interests, the continuous changes of place and circulation of cadres also occurred in these institutions (Csanádi, 1987). As a result of these movements, a refined network of contacts evolved among those in power, with their way of life and values converging. A most important feature of their common ethos was the *sense of privilege* described as follows by Tamás Bauer (1982):

> "The mechanism of the command economy had created an elite of economic management forged from former 'professional revolutionaries,' technicians, 'planning bureaucrats,' old and new 'captains of industry' (including worker-

managers). This elite, in its totality rather than its parts, had become the agent of 'rational redistribution.' The stratum as a whole had evolved a specific messianic consciousness of being the transformers of the economy and society (into something professional), which was reflected in the fact that it was they who made all the economic decisions, free of any social control, either on the part of political democracy, or on that of the market mechanism."

Based on the above, I consider the owners of power in 'existing socialism,' in Max Weber's terms, as a *status group with some traits of a class*, and will call them the *status group in power*. It was a status group by virtue of intra-group relations and because its power originally was not of an economic nature, but it possessed class features because its power was becoming increasingly economic, as was tested in the market, albeit at a low level. The status group in power had interests that were definitely separate from those of the society, and it was able to assert those interests.

The next question is that of ownership: can the category of ownership be applied at all when describing the power relations of 'existing socialism'? If one sets out from the economic and sociological concept of ownership, the essence of which is the right of disposal (Sárközy, 1982), then the answer is undoubtedly yes: according to every relevant piece of empirical research, it was primarily the status group in power that had the right of disposal over anything called social or state property. In addition it held not only the rights of disposal, but, at least in certain periods, also the rights of operation (down to the minutest day-to-day decisions), as well as receiving a far greater than average share of the profits of the so-called social or state property (Bence–Kis, 1983; Szalai 1989b; Fehér–Heller–Márkus, 1991). Although the members of the status group in power could not bequeath any ownership rights directly to their descendants, it can be stated, with the concepts of Bourdieu (1983) in mind, that they could transfer much greater than average cultural and social capital (or more exactly, the ability to acquire it) to their children, who, in their turn would be able to convert it even into economic capital. (More about this later.)

Therefore the power structure showed class traits not only in the Weberian, but also in the Marxian sense: the status group in power collectively possessed almost all the ownership rights. As this ownership was a diffuse and momentary one, it provoked constant struggles, the aim of which was the acquisition of as many rights as possible and the avoidance and shifting of as much responsibility as possible (Szalai, 1989b, 1991, 2001). Ferenc Fehér – Ágnes Heller – György Márkus (1991) hold a similar view: "We have characterized the basic economic condition of Soviet-type societies as one in which the apparatus of power is in corporate possession of the objective means of social production, from which labor has not been totally separated."

The last half sentence quoted leads us to the concrete relationship between power and society, but by way of introduction I must make a slight detour.

On the one hand, I must explain why I define the power structure as merely a conglomerate with class traits and not as a class. I do so above all because that part of the society which was outside its power structure—in relation to certain factors to be presented shortly—was not organized into a class, and there is no society with one class only. In the post-Stalinist period no class struggle in the Marxian sense was in progress within 'existing socialism' (with the exception of Poland), whereas one of the essential points of Marxian class theory, which I regard as the most relevant, is that the classes (sooner or later) 'acquire' their existence and form in their conflicts and struggles. (This essentially derives from Marx's assumption that the class struggle is the most decisive engine of incessant societal development. I have some problems with this assumption and I shall come back to it.)

On the other hand, I have to reflect on the theses of György Bencze – János Kis and Ferenc Fehér – Ágnes Heller – György Márkus concerning ownership relations. Their shared view is that the power conglomerate of 'existing socialism' operated the means of production on the basis of motivations and criteria that were totally different from those of individual capitalists working in the capitalist system, and the relationship of that conglomerate to the means of production was determined by the logic of politics and power, and not by that of profitable production. In other words, here the motivation of economic decisions was the stabilization and extension of political power and not the desire to ensure and enhance efficiency measured by profit. György Bencze and János Kis draw the conclusion that the existing power conglomerate was not the owner of the means of production, and Ferenc Fehér – Ágnes Heller – György Márkus, speaking about the ownership position of the conglomerate, stress vigorously the difference between it and capitalist ownership.

I, for my part, feel that the difference between the ownership relations of 'existing socialism' and capitalism are far less marked. The power conglomerate, particularly in the Stalinist period of 'existing socialism,' actually exercised a "dictatorship of modernization" (Iván Berend T.), in which it was obliged for a long time to dispense with the inclusion of short-term market signals, short-term efficiency and profitability in economic decisions. Based on Gerschenkron's (1984) theory, it can be argued that semi-feudal conditions, economic backwardness, and the resultant need to catch up entailed the emergence of a strong central power here as in other societies with similar conditions. (This is the point of view of functionalism, as opposed to the approach of conflict theory applied by me so far.) In addition to hard power considerations, there was a decisive (and real) demand to establish an industrial society, which, requiring the radical breaking-up of the old societal and economic structure and the building of a brand new one, almost totally excluded any considerations of efficiency of a market type suited for managing a more balanced and shorter-term resource allocation. More exactly: considerations deriving from the need for modernization became the efficiency criteria of the proprietorial decisions of the power conglomerate—with the emphasis on 'proprietorial.' What may be their results in the long run—how 'effective' they may prove in a historical perspective—is to be answered by this book as a whole.

The dividing line between 'existing socialism' and capitalism was also made less sharp, as described earlier, by the way the managers of big companies during the post-Stalinist period of 'existing socialism' became part of the power, so that, counter to popular understanding, the power was not only a political one, but was increasingly based on the economy and acquired an 'economic nature.' This cannot be separated from the fact that the crisis of the economy—particularly in the post-Stalinist period, when economic expansion met efficiency barriers of a market type—forced the technocrats of the party state or state party to incorporate more and more efficiency criteria into the decision-making mechanisms of redistribution. A good example is provided by the fact that when the fifth five-year plan was drawn up in Hungary in the mid-1970s, in addition to the natural 'supply tasks,' including 'socialist' exports, the efficiency and 'profitability' of exports to the West played an outstanding role in the bargaining process between the 'governing organizations' and the managers of big companies—in other words, this consideration was an important element of state redistribution already at that time, and its significance has continued to grow since (Szalai, 1989b). In parallel to this process, the economic reforms which created increasing space for the market elements, presented earlier, also became inevitable (Bauer, 1982).

To conclude: in the post-Stalinist period the status group in power, with significant differences between different countries, was beginning increasingly to resemble capitalist private owners. I may add that this applies not only to its decisions, but also to its values and way of life.

CHAPTER 2

# Power and Society

## SPECIFICITIES OF THE RELATIONSHIP BETWEEN CAPITAL AND LABOR

The last train of thought leads to the issue of exploitation: the concentration of ownership rights and the exploitative relationship as the source of that concentration, according to those criteria by which I myself interpret exploitation (Szalai, 2001). Essentially one may speak about exploitation (with certain restrictions) when it can be proven that there is a high degree of inequality between the respective bargaining positions of the 'labor side' and the 'capital side,' which is used by the 'capital side' continuously to strengthen its position in every respect to the detriment of the 'labor side.' It was this situation that emerged in 'existing socialism,' under which the workforce was exploited in wage labor, with the special feature that, in contrast to capitalist societies, the 'labor side' was not unambiguously separate from the 'capital side' and their conflicting interests were not articulated, because, to use a commonly known expression, the "workers were nationalized." After an initial phase of terror and forced 'centralization,' it was the atomized and informal assertion of interests that increasingly became the decisive factor and the workers' chief mode of interest assertion within the hierarchical system. Its most important aim and means was '*integration by one leg*' into the various levels or channels of the hierarchy, which promised special treatment and at the same time the possibility of maintaining an '*individualized, limited, and relative autonomy.*' The individuals were structured according to how far they were able and striving to develop their relative autonomy while constantly keeping their hierarchical contacts in good order.

It was not by accident that Zsuzsa Ferge (1969), in her analysis of the social structure of 'existing socialism,' raised the question whether the separate strata are nominal or real groups, and whether we can speak about group relations or only about a collection of individuals with identical characteristics. On the same basis, in 1989 I formulated my own thesis that it was more accurate to speak merely about social strata and not social groups in 'existing socialism.'

The fact that individuals advanced predominantly by the assertion of their interests through the channels of the various levels of the hierarchy usually *meant the lack of the possibility of collective and open interest assertion and at the same time the lack of concern for it.* The political institutions limited the assertion of partial interests from the bottom up, while precedents of the success of individual bargains were constantly emerging and the patterns of collective behavior socially recognized as successful were missing. It is an important example of the lack of concern that the appearance and subsequent expansion of the second economy offered the choice of alternative life strategies to certain social strata, while it was precisely the opportunities offered by the second economy that absorbed the individual ambitions of those who could have articulated the interests of the strata or groups concerned. Thus the social pressure necessary for the creation of independent organizations to assert group interests was missing. The individuals (as well as the economic organizations) were *structured* in accordance with the *extent of the role played by the lack of possibility and concern in the absence of any organized expression of partial interests initiated from the bottom.* (For instance, it would have been downright disadvantageous for the managers of big companies to express their separate interests unambiguously in an organized form, because one of their basic means of interest assertion was to make it appear in the garb of a more general interest than their own.) Those strata pushed to the periphery of society and excluded from the opportunity for atomized interest assertion, such as the pensioners and the unemployed, should have been particularly involved in the organizational articulation, from the bottom up, of their interests, but they were incapable either of truly recognizing this or of putting it into practice. With some simplification one may say that those who, given their position and their opportunities of interest assertion, had a really good chance of creating autonomous interest organizations did not need these, while those who needed them were in a weak position and did not have the means to do so.

Consequently *no other class or status group was organized against the status group in power.* That is why it happened—and why it could happen—that the relationship between 'capital' and 'labor' was marked by inequality and a grave imbalance to the benefit of capital and the detriment of labor.

## THE COMPLEX NATURE OF SOCIETAL RELATIONS

The features of the power structure outlined above add up to a state capitalist, more exactly a state and big-company capitalist, system. (The characterization of 'existing socialism' as a state capitalist system has significant antecedents in the literature [see primarily Cliff, 1974]; however, the thesis of the prominent power position of the managers of big companies is the result of my own researches.) At the same time, various socialistic processes were taking place within the system. One of these was large-scale social mobility roughly up to the early 1980s. Another, related to the first, was the significant cultural upliftment of broad social strata. Finally, as a result of these processes, a heterogeneous 'middle class,' unique at least in Hungarian social development, was born: its aims were modest but accessible and could be calculated with certainty (a prefabricated flat, a small wooden cottage on a river bank, a Trabant car). Those were the social developments that gave the system a socialist tinge. (And as a result of these developments, 'existing socialism' represented a serious challenge to the entire capitalist world. Without this challenge the post-World War II welfare states might not have come into being, and this is perhaps the most significant achievement of 'existing socialism.')

At the same time, it should be noted that although the socialistic traits outlined were not independent of the official ideology of the status group in power, they rarely derived from the commitment of that status group to the people, or from performance of its duty. Nor did they derive from the democratically won social rights of the people, and even less from their ownership rights. Rather, as mentioned earlier, social relations were essentially determined by the fact that the status group in power compensated for its missing political legitimacy by the continuous rise of living standards and the tolerated development of the second economy. To put it differently: the continuous rise of living standards and the opening of the channels of the second economy, while it lasted and was 'efficient,' was nothing but a way of allowing part of the surplus value to be transferred to the society in order to maintain political stability (or to be somewhat provocative, the 'price of silence'). This was the only way of ensuring—as long as it could be ensured—the legitimacy of the system and the power structure in a sociological sense. In fact, one of the decisive causes of the exhaustion of the system, to be dealt with later, was that the economic possibilities for the continuous rise of living standards (and also the opportunities hidden in the second economy as part of this) were drying up in the entire region by the late 1970s (Bauer, 1982).

Apart from ideological aims, serious power motivations may also be discovered for the reduction and active diminution of social inequalities as compared to pre-World War II conditions.

According to Zsuzsa Ferge (2002), "more or less everything concerning the destiny of freedom can be predicted from the dictatorial nature of power relations, but nothing follows in respect of the development of inequalities." I wish to challenge this statement from two angles. On the one hand, I believe that as a consequence of the post-Stalinist power structure of 'existing socialism' and its legitimacy in the sociological sense of the term—in other words, their (at least passive) acceptance by the majority of society (with the exception of Poland)—*must be regarded as a paternalist, authoritarian system, rather than a dictatorship.* On the other hand, the continuous alleviation of inequalities by the status group in power was also motivated (not necessarily consciously) by the concern that no rival, potentially 'power-ready,' groups should form against it, and no social strata threatened by declining fortunes should become the starting point and base of a possible 'class struggle' under the given conditions. Therefore the status group in power had serious power interests in relatively equitable conditions of distribution in an economic as well as cultural sense. (This was in contrast to 'developed' capitalism, which ensures the political legitimacy of the power conglomerates by means of political rotation and which, located at the center of the world economy, is economically strong and therefore able to give a share of its extra profits to its own working class, so that the great inequalities do not directly endanger the stability of the system.)

Thus an incompatible 'middle class' emerged in 'existing socialism' *as a result of an unbalanced petty-bourgeois development.* According to Júlia Szalai (1988), the essential feature of this imbalance was that "only one half of the petty-bourgeois development, accumulation with the aim of *consumption*, based on self-exploitation, was compatible with the unquestioned power structure."

György Bencze and János Kis (1983) hold a partly different view, seeing the advance of consumer values and the expansion of the possibilities of individual consumption as an opportunity—without a real alternative—for the emergence and strengthening of individual autonomy: "in a Soviet-type society, social activity is coordinated and controlled by a set of institutions which makes any kind of self-organization impossible, and which, in normal circumstances, reduces the resistance of workers to individual actions. In such conditions the accumulation of privately owned goods is not the alternative to the only possible—that is, individual—autonomy, but the means of achieving it. The worker with some economic backing can more easily resist his superior and better ride out temporary losses when he voluntarily or forcibly changes his place of work."

A 'further developed' variant of this point of view appeared in the discussion of the Hungarian democratic opposition and Hungarian reform economists with István Csurka at the Monor meeting of 1985. According to Csurka, the advance of consumer demand signified the abandonment of comprehensive societal aims (essentially the betrayal of the 1956 revolution), bringing with it continuous moral degradation. In contrast, the representatives of the democratic opposition and the reform economists argued that since the 1956 revolution—and, so to speak, as its achievement—we had been witnessing an ascending social process in which small, individual autonomies, emerging on the basis of advancing consumption, increasingly became organic ones, and were expanded, linked and institutionalized, as it were laying the foundations for eventual political autonomy. (Minutes of the Monor meeting. Manuscript, 1985. This was the first public meeting of Hungarian marginal intellectuals.)

In 1985, I agreed with the latter point of view but, given the 'historical perspective' that has developed since, I now believe that it is rather the stance of Bence and Kis (1983) that reflected the real conditions: the expansion of the opportunities of individual consumption was indeed the sole base of individual autonomy in 'existing socialism.' But it should be stressed that it was the base of individual autonomy alone, because it counteracted the demands for those community autonomies that could be achieved jointly. Nevertheless, the continuous growth of consumer expectations (for which 'existing socialism' provided the necessary socialization) ultimately led to the disintegration of the system, although this was the result of entirely different mechanisms than the transformation of consumer autonomies into a political one. (I shall return to this question later.)

The significance of the market mechanism, closely linked to consumption, may be assessed in similarly contradictory terms. András Hegedűs (1969), Ota Sik (1972), György Bencze – János Kis (1978) and Ferenc Fehér – Ágnes Heller – György Márkus (1992) all believe that the market mechanism appearing within the framework of 'existing socialism' was able to loosen the rigid hierarchy of the power structure and therefore not only to expand the opportunities for individual freedom, but also to make societal control over the power conglomerate possible in the long run. In reality, it was evident—at least in the first phase of the post-Stalinist period, roughly up to the middle of the 1970s—that the appearance of the market elements actually stabilized and conserved the system by making the operation of the power mechanism smoother (Szalai, 1989b). All this was not independent of the fact, proven by the researches of Iván Szelényi and Eric Kostello (1996), that the primary manifestations of the market reduced, rather than increased, the social inequalities at the beginning of the post-Stalinist period. The decisive reason, also pointed out by Viktor Nee (1991), was that the appearance of market elements, while not eliminating the privileges of the 'cadres,' weakened them to some extent. Finally, although the further development and expansion of the market mechanism—not least by promoting the growth of inequalities in the second phase of the post-Stalinist period—broke up the framework of 'existing socialism,' this was not the result of a revival of broad social activity. Nor was it independent of the fact that the 'market,' in contrast to the ideas of the authors quoted, did not operate in a self-regulatory way: it did not grant everybody free entry into its space, and only the demand side was strengthened, while the supply side failed to catch up, because it was dominated by the big companies in monopoly positions intent on holding back their output, and by the technocracy guarding its power and consumer interests. (This is another question to which I shall return later.)

## "To Become External and Alien"

Marx introduced the concept of estrangement for the critical analysis of capitalist society, but the phenomenon described by him also applies precisely to the social conditions of 'existing socialism.' According to Marx (1977), "Estrangement is manifested not only in the fact that *my* means of life belong to *someone* else, that which *I* desire is the inaccessible possession of *another*, but also in the fact that everything is itself something *different* from itself—that my activity is *something else* and that, finally (and this applies also to the capitalists), all is under the sway of *inhuman* power."

In what follows I will discuss Marx's points one by one.

"*My* means of life belong to *someone* else." Earlier I tried to prove that in 'existing socialism' the means of production were owned by the status group in power, whose interests were definitely separate from those of society, while, in contrast to capitalist societies, the ' labor side' was not visibly separate from the power conglomerate and for that reason (among others) had no chance of openly and collectively articulating and representing its interests against the conglomerate.

"That which *I* desire is the inaccessible possession of *another*." György Bencze and János Kis (1978), quoting Marx, argue as follows: "Profit is indifferent towards everything that is not reflected in the transformations of the exchange relations. Therefore the efforts to increase profits do not coincide with the efforts to satisfy the demands of producers and consumers. Marx called this systematic discrepancy estrangement. A similar difference, however, is caused by the indices of success set for Soviet-type companies." Subsequently Bencze and Kis prove in detail that the indices of success mediate between social needs and the production sphere far less effectively than does capitalist profit. They then state: "The capitalist company is part of a self-regulatory mechanism, which more or less continuously adjusts profit to at least part of the changing technical possibilities and social needs: to that part which manifests itself in production costs and solvent demand. In this area it is the market that limits the distortions of the profit rate, but only in this area. There are technical possibilities and social needs to which the profit rate does not react. In such cases the feedback from the market does not reduce the distortions, but enhances them. Nevertheless, the Soviet-type solution of the problem is not a good one. *It does not eliminate estrangement: what it eliminates is the feedback mechanism that keeps estrangement within limits.*" (Italics mine, E. Sz.)

The title of a book on 'existing socialism' by Ferenc Fehér – Ágnes Heller – György Márkus (1991) is *Dictatorship over Needs*. This recalls Marx's "that which *I* desire is the inaccessible possession of *another*."

These authors again exaggerate the disparity between 'existing socialism' and capitalism. They do so primarily because, by regarding the market operating under capitalism as self-regulatory, they idealize both the market and the related role of the fluctuations of the profit rate. In reality we know that, on the one hand, the existence of large monopolies interested in holding back their supply is a feature not only of 'existing socialism,' but also of capitalism, and that, on the other hand, the power conglomerate of capitalism is also capable of strongly influencing needs, not by open dictatorship, but by partly deliberate and partly unconscious manipulation. Nevertheless, in the period when capitalism had an alternative in 'existing socialism,' the capitalist market and the fluctuations of profit rates responded more effectively to social needs and 'estranged' them less than did central planning and regulation.

"Everything is itself something *different* from itself." In 'existing socialism' a wide gap separated the officially declared and desired values from those that were followed in real life. As Ágnes Losonczi (1977) writes: "All this [the lack of opportunity for individual and collective self-determination – E. Sz.] overturns and dissolves formerly solid values: uncertainty develops between the reality and the socially accepted or commended values. Orientation becomes difficult, because people live by adjusting to their circumstances, and not according to the declarations of values and texts which, lacking confirmation by practice, make adjustment difficult."

One of the main declared values of 'existing socialism' was the community spirit (and several representatives of the status group in power were actually convinced that they were serving and representing the community by their activities). In reality, however, the "community society" granted only very limited and 'specific' functions to the communities. The authorities tolerated the existence of those communities alone that behaved like a compliant herd of sheep—communities which in no way and at no level challenged the legitimacy of the existing system or even that of their immediate superiors, and which in exchange received favors doled out from the top. In addition there were some apparent communities established from above, which strongly restricted and controlled the individuals belonging to them.

This is how Ferenc Erős (1988) describes the situation:
"The disintegration of the small communities that had supplied a medium and a background for the normal and balanced functioning of the personality took place under conditions in which 'small communities' were officially declared dangerous. The greatest enemy of the system advocating a collectivist ideology was seen to be the collective, i.e. the spontaneously evolving small community. As Ferenc Mérei said in an interview entitled 'I have no abstract message': 'The Rákosi regime regarded most forms of human coexistence as cliques.' A frightening example of the consequences of this outlook—still effective today—was the way some teachers carried out 'sociometric surveys' in their classes in order to identify the kinds of 'cliques' that had evolved among the children and to 'eliminate' as promptly as they could any 'cliques' that they were able to find. One of the long-term consequences of the liquidation of small communities (associations, groups, nonhierarchical organizations, etc.) was that the private sphere almost totally retreated to the family, so that the family became the venue of every nonofficial activity, including leisure and entertainment, and civil society was replaced by the Orwellian symbiosis of family and television. Thus the family had such burdens loaded on it—in addition to the existing ones—as it should not, or at least not primarily, be expected to bear. Naturally the small

communities could not be eliminated, because it is a basic fact of social psychology that people are inclined to organize themselves 'informally' even in the shadow of the most rigid formal groups and institutions. But, when free and democratic communities are missing, such 'a-legal' groups become marginal and deviant, or are officially regarded as such; at other times they become an invisible lobby, a secret and uncontrollable decision-making body (when, for instance, important political issues are decided on a hunting trip)."

This is how all the phenomena I have described became dominant in 'existing socialism': essentially they add up to a widespread individual, atomized, and informal bargaining process, in which every individual tried above all else to make a private deal with his or her immediate superior. The changes undergone by 'existing socialism' can also be explained by this approach. The first, dictatorial period could be replaced—in Hungary after the 1956 revolution—by a 'soft dictatorship' because of the deals mentioned above: the employees and the citizens in general renounced the exercise of political freedom, initially in order to obtain a share in the benefits coming from the center, and then in order to be able to withdraw increasingly into the second economy and second society (the size of which was different in each country).

As expounded by Elemér Hankiss (1984), in 'existing socialism' civil society—in the sense of a space for "communication free of domination" (Habermas, no date)—was *different* in that it appeared as the second society: "the mechanisms, structures, and institutions of civil society did not, and could not, develop even within the second society, because the external pressure was extremely high, and therefore even in this sphere of civil society only a fragmentary element, a pale experiment, an 'as-if existence' could be observed." Thus, as Hankiss sees it, the position of civil society in 'existing socialism' was highly vulnerable and its significance very small.

Although the idealization of a concept—that of civil society in this instance—is also characteristic of Hankiss's theory, his approach sensitively indicates the system's 'lack of communities' and the weakness of its democratic structures.

These conditions are connected with the strong presence of the authoritarian principle and authoritarian psychic structures, as opposed to the officially proclaimed ideas of equality, leveling, and continuous democratization.

To quote Ferenc Erős (1988):
"The generations currently alive were, without exception, brought up in totalitarian and dictatorial, or at least authoritarian and paternalist systems, and their socialization took place in such a medium—('Under the spell of violence,' as Attila József wrote). Those in their thirties and forties today have lived since their birth or childhood in a system which has been symbolized by the name of the same leader and in which the same questions have remained taboo.

Naturally, the authoritarianism of political power is bound to affect the structure of the personality; it is mediated by formal and informal institutions and the 'agents of socialization,' such as public opinion, ideology, mass communications, school, and, to some extent, even the family. As demonstrated by the psychoanalytical social psychology of the 30s and 40s (Wilhelm Reich, Fromm, Adorno, etc.) authoritarian power and the authoritarian personality presuppose and build on each other. This is not to say that everybody would necessarily become an 'authoritarian personality' under conditions of authoritarian power. But even those people whose thinking shows no trace of authoritarianism and who were lucky enough to be able to identify with alternative models in the course of their personality development usually lack the necessary familiarity with democracy and their social experience is dominated by a sense of hierarchies, inferiority or superiority, and the immobility and unalterability of things. The authoritarian solution is ready-made and socially accepted at every level of life; the democratic, 'decentring' solution, based on mutuality, is rare, exceptional and often regarded as 'deviant' in itself. Sometimes it is the lack of authoritarianism that leads to psychological disturbance, because in the absence of democracy—or at least of tolerance—being 'different' is a stigma, and the person thus stigmatized may seek the fault in himself, which, in turn, may be a source of anxiety and a sense of guilt. The reverse of autocracy is anarchy, total laissez faire, and where crystallized democratic principles are missing, either one side or another will assert itself, unless both become effective jointly in the form of 'organized irresponsibility.' The autocracy that accompanies anarchy, upheaval, disorder, and the mystification of responsibility, together with the opacity and impermeability of everything, has been well known to East and Central Europeans, at least since the time of Franz Kafka."

Rather than the advancement of communitarianism and democratization, the broad social strata deprived of power in 'existing socialism' regarded a quiet private life, continuous economic accumulation, and the expansion of a limited autonomy as the supreme value (Simon, 1994). *Relative autonomy*, a complex and unbalanced principle marked by internal contradictions, was at the center of the period's value system, from the apex of power down to the lowest social strata. It represented the adaptability, deriving from multiple linkages, that held the social structure of 'existing socialism' together—until its growing internal tensions and the exhaustion of its inherent possibilities signaled its crisis.

"My activity is *something else.*" It was primarily István Kemény (1972) who demonstrated how forced industrialization in the 1950s led to *inorganic mobility.* The most decisive feature and consequence of this process was that the status of workers in their workplace and their home—and, as a result, their identity—became largely uncertain. A corollary of this process was massive and increasing loneliness. Inorganic mobility, as stressed by Ágnes Losonczi (1989), was perhaps the most decisive factor, not mentioned so far, of the disastrous lack of communities and the dominance of individual and informal interest assertion.

In this context István Kemény characterizes the situation of Hungarian workers as follows:

"The closed culture of the previous generation of workers is disintegrating: today's Hungarian workers are no longer a closed social stratum with solid customs and clear-cut interrelationships, but rather a huge camp of travelers. Some of them are peasants who have become, or are becoming, workers and who lead transitory lives between the village and the city, between a peasant's and a worker's habits. And even those who were born workers are on their way from the worker in the old sense to a new type. Some become group leaders, foremen, technicians, or engineers; others join factory laboratories or servicing workshops; yet others take odd jobs and spend the most important part of their lives outside the factory; in any case the majority of them lose touch with a traditional way of life... The gravest problem, however, is definitely the loss of the old bonds and customs, which may result in a lack of partner, loneliness, and internal uncertainty. The old rural way of life bound and held the individual too much, not only restricting his or her happiness and freedom, but often even causing neuroses. The urban way of life, according to many social scientists, is characterized by the other extreme: it leaves the individual alone too much, thus causing material and emotional uncertainty. If there is any truth in this statement, it applies primarily to those who have come to town from the villages: they lack live human relations most of all, because they have generally lost the old ones and find it extremely difficult to acquire new ones on alien soil."

Ágnes Losonczi notes:

"When a fairly broad stratum, as a result of accumulating some wealth and rising above the level of poverty, had acquired self-confidence, it became less interested in building the community than in strengthening individualism—and the desire to protect a temporarily improved situation impairs mutual patience and the will to help one another."

A radical change in status and identity, accompanied by growing loneliness, also means that the individual feels totally exposed to the 'big' social forces and processes he or she is unable to comprehend. Losonczi (1977) quotes the following passage from her interview with an unskilled worker aged 52: "One's life is governed by forces one can't interfere with. No matter how one plans, if something happens, politics, war, everything will be different." According to an empirical survey carried out by Losonczi at the time, "the fact that human beings constantly depend on the operation of forces they cannot interfere with, influence, or perhaps even always understand—this experience plays a very strong part when [the interviewees – E. Sz.] speak about the development of their guiding principles."

"Finally (and this applies also to the capitalists), all is under the sway of *inhuman* power." At the dawn of 'existing socialism,' as already indicated, several members of the status group in power were capable of forming truly positive identities and therefore internally experienced ideologies of legitimacy. All this evaporated in the fully developed phase of the system. To quote András Lányi (1988): "The elite of office-holders that evolved around the institutions and leading positions of social and economic management is undergoing a crisis of legitimacy. According to their own ideology, they should have a revolutionary-socialist sense of belonging to the worker and peasant class, but their position and entire function make it impossible for them to consider themselves as revolutionaries, workers, or peasants, while the ideology legitimizing the order of the society forbids them to regard themselves as an elite. At any rate, they identify with the leading bodies only with significant restrictions… The leading stratum therefore has no solid sense of identity."

Thus the status group in power dominates, but is also at the mercy of, the existing power relations. This perhaps is the most conspicuous sign of the estranged nature of the entire system.

To sum up, it may not be too strong a statement that 'existing socialism' socialized people into passivity, servility, and slyness in relation to estranged conditions, and that we suffer the consequences to this day. Not a single Western or Eastern transitologist foresaw in the early 1990s what was to come: how the population of the postsocialist countries tolerated, practically without saying a word, the enormous syphoning of incomes that was the reality behind the "original regrouping of capital" and the huge social burden resulting from it—unprecedented unemployment hitting almost every family, a marked and sudden growth of the mortality rate (Szamuely, 1995), and many other things that could be listed.

CHAPTER 3

# The Issue of Interest Integration

In contrast to capitalist societies, where the particular societal interests are decisively confronted and integrated by the market, in the developed phase of 'existing socialism' this function was primarily performed by the status group in power and the technocracy, in other words, the state party and party state.

## THE COMMAND ECONOMY

The history of this system of interest integration began in the strict command economy prevailing at the time. In the traditional command economy, market bargaining—which is apt to reconcile partial interests horizontally and which presupposes (at least partial) public accountancy—is rejected, with the result that partial interests surface with elemental force in the course of *plan bargaining*, which becomes increasingly complex and involves a growing number of actors. The power conglomerate tried to control the economic units by increasing the number of hierarchical dependencies, but this was precisely the reason why it gradually lost its control over the economic processes. The growing number of dependencies, which meant a growing complexity of hierarchical relationships, in reality enhanced maneuvering ability of the economic units.

A more general cause of the loss of dominance can be found in the specificities of the political mechanism. In the given political system, which offered no opportunity for the development of alternative life programs, the only possible way of achieving individual success was by adjusting to the power hierarchy. This atomized the society and prevented the emergence of different communities that could have exercised effective political control over the power conglomerate (Hankiss, 1983).

The hierarchy of the power institutions may be considered as an administrative system designed for the suppression of partial interests. It did not exclude frequent acts of suppression carried out in the name of elevating some assumed or real partial interests—for instance those of the 'working class'—to a political rank. But there could be no total suppression, and various partial interests actually tried to manifest and assert themselves in the garb of societal interests or political significance. As a result, the real articulation of society remained hidden from the power conglomerate, which increasingly damaged the 'effectiveness' of the measures taken by it. In the 1950s, this Stalinist-type social and economic establishment found itself in crisis and collapsed.

## INTEREST INTEGRATION IN THE POST-STALINIST PERIOD

The reform experiments of the 1960s arose from the demand for the stabilization of control over societal and economic processes and as a result of the related insights which led to the emergence of a new model, called *indirect economic mechanism* (Antal, 1985). The essence of this mechanism was its *incongruity*, resulting from the extremely uncertain economic position of individuals and the ownership entitlements of economic organizations.

The indirect economic mechanism was part of the *indirect socio-economic mechanism*. Compared to the earlier period, in this system the constraints on individuals and economic organizations decreased, but the evolution of full autonomy was hindered by publicly declared or, to a large extent, informally asserted restrictions. While the role of horizontal contacts and the market grew and the second economy expanded, the relationship between individuals and economic organizations, on the one hand, and the various levels of the hierarchy, on the other, continued to be the most important. As a consequence of the primacy of hierarchical relations and the survival of dependency, atomized interest assertion remained the dominant path of achievement. The coalitions and interest alliances that occasionally emerged were transitory and easily upset; nor did they usually aim at institutionalization, but rather tried to achieve their objectives informally.

The economic organizations still continued as *quasi-enterprises*, and the position of their managers was characterized by contradictions: meeting the requirements of the market often clashed with the expectations of the various units of the state party and party state (Bauer, 1975). Nor were the representatives of the state and party united: the functional governing organizations voiced mainly financial demands, while those of the branches demanded mainly natural produce (i.e. specific goods).

The structure of the industry remained strongly centralized, and the large companies that held key positions as organic and indispensable elements of the economy were able to syphon off incomes for themselves from other areas of the economy through the central institutions (Szalai 1989b). The large companies created by the direct mechanism of management appeared as autonomous interest centers in the indirect mechanism of management. There was a mismatch between the decision-making system, which was characteristic of the indirect economic mechanism after the economic reforms, and the hierarchy of the central institutions and their links to the economic sphere. Behind the monolithic appearance of the power conglomerate, a *constantly changing* system of subordination, superordination, and coordination evolved. The *regularly recurring* conflicts and compromises between the institutions dealing with issues of branches, areas, and companies (primarily the branch ministries) during that period of constant change were also 'real' conflicts and compromises between branches, areas, and companies (or groups of companies). The top economic management and the functional institutions strongly influenced the course of those conflicts and compromises. In fact, they themselves created conflicts, but all the time they had to take into account the fact that the power relations of the other institutions in contact with them also *reflected broader economic and power relations*. Thus we are faced with a *contradictory phenomenon*: the interest conflicts of *relatively autonomous economic and political subjects and their groups* were expressed and solved through the channels of a system built mainly on *subordination and superordination* (Szalai, 1989b; Grossman, 1992).

If we interpret the phrase "relatively autonomous economic and political subjects and their groups" more broadly, and if we include the "societal groups" and interest organizations that have a specific overlapping relationship with the branches, areas, and companies, then the features of the decision-making mechanism outlined above actually amount to the so-called *system of interest inclusion*. To quote Mihály Bihari (1985): "After 1956 we took significant steps towards democratizing the political system, interest representation, and the exercise of power. Today the party and state apparatus understands and incorporates more sensitively the movement of interests emerging in society... As a result, our current political system and decision-making mechanism are in a better position to take into account the interests and differences of opinion existing in society. However, on the whole, our political system today is not yet capable of institutionally and publicly including the differences of interest and opinion in the decision-making mechanism." László Bruszt (1987) puts it in similar terms: "It was not possible to create separate mechanisms to institutionalize the interests and desires of the different social groups, but within the institutional system of governance itself irregular mechanisms of mediation from the bottom up have been emerging. The key word is 'interest inclusion.'"

The concept of interest inclusion simultaneously contained elements of an *ex-ante* consciousness and a sense of direct coercion. This meant that the individuals organized in the power conglomerate, on the one hand, *recognized* the *general* need to consider partial interests, while, on the other hand, they *were forced* to include those partial interests in their calculations of the conditions of asserting their own interests in *particular concrete situations*.

László Antal (1985) characterizes direct coercion as follows:
"It is also a fact that in the wake of these changes a mechanism is taking shape that requires less the limitation of partial interests (of individuals, groups, stra-

ta, and organizations) in order to assert central objectives; indeed, as an indispensable part of that mechanism, the participants in top-level decision-making may come to reckon with the reactions of subordinate organizations not participating in decision-making, and even with their silent—but extremely effective—resistance."

Elemér Hankiss (1984) called this phenomenon latent pluralism. "Latent pluralism is not democratic participation in power but a pluralism of the possibilities of influencing power. Political science speaks about 'influence' when a social stratum or group which has no possibility of participating in decisions or controlling their implementation, is somehow able to assert its interests by exercising an influence on decisions. It can do so because it owns some resources or goods which are needed by the whole society or by the governing elite, and which cannot be mobilized by open violence or could be mobilized only at the cost of disproportionately heavy losses."

The operation of the mechanism of interest inclusion from the point of view of the interests of the power conglomerate—in other words, *governability*—may be called efficient if the operation of the power conglomerate in relation to the partial interests manifest in society can be shown to be dominated by *ex-ante* consciousness. This means that the state party and party state has been capable of recognizing and incorporating partial interests in response to relatively small direct pressure. On the other hand, partial interests of one kind or another could not be allowed to become totally dominant. Thus there had to be the possibility of counterbalancing any pressure groups in too strong positions by pushing some weaker groups into the foreground. Seen from the aspect of society and *social justice*, the effective operation of the mechanism of interest inclusion depended on the economic and political subjects or groups being granted equal opportunities for asserting their interests at the center of power. (At this point I do not wish to analyze in depth the extremely complicated relationship between governability and social justice. Nevertheless, it may be noted that there were issues in which the requirements of the two points of view strengthened, rather than excluded, each other. To take a concrete example: it was not desirable from either point of view that significant—potentially conflicting—societal groups should be able to call the attention of the power conglomerate to themselves at the cost of being seriously degraded. In other words, in analyzing the operation of the mechanism of interest inclusion we may assume right from the outset that in a variety of issues we may not end by identifying contradictions.)

By the mid-1980s, the mechanism of interest inclusion found itself in open crisis, the reason being that, in terms of the features listed above, it had never really functioned efficiently. In fact, it was so far from operating efficiently that we may even ask whether *the object of our investigation can truly be considered as a mechanism of interest inclusion*. In what follows I wish to examine this question by analyzing those factors that made the efficient operation of the mechanism of interest inclusion impossible.

As we have seen, the question is above all whether the power conglomerate was able to develop an idea of the actual political and economic articulation of the society that corresponded to the reality. László Bruszt (1987) points out that the political actors were primarily institutions and not societal groups. Elemér Hankiss (1984) says: "The existing set of institutions neither fits nor suits the system of social interests." I myself have shown that in 'existing socialism' social groups existed only in name.

Another reason for the difficulty of seeing the system clearly, as indicated by Mária Csanádi (1987), was the extremely complicated internal structure of the power conglomerate, "an incomprehensible basic web," as she calls it. In my view, it lacked adequate lucidity, and agreements between its actors came about mostly through informal bargains, with every participant having a vested interest in maintaining this situation.

The inadequate lucidity of the power conglomerate's internal power relations in itself made it almost incapable of faithfully reflecting the real societal power relations. On the other hand, this deficiency constantly reproduced the uncertainty of power relations within the conglomerate. In Mária Csanádi's words: "each actor (decision-maker) was followed as well as confronted by a phantom crowd: his popular base was as large as he could make others believe, or as large as he himself wanted to or was forced to believe... Therefore the bargaining position of the actors, whether similar or conflicting, was always uncertain, variable on each occasion and 'momentary.' It was momentary even if it seemed relatively stable: one had to struggle and to maintain or reestablish contacts continuously, which required constant watchfulness and adjustment."

The reflection of the real divisions within the societal interest relations was restricted by another factor—closely related to the previous one—i.e. the way the institutions of the power conglomerate directly sensed the interests and objectives of their economic and political subjects and the differences between these. In what follows I will approach only the economic organizations from this angle.

The power conglomerate's prime means of identifying the interests and objectives of economic organizations was the synthesis of individual bargains struck with them, which had several consequences. On the one hand, the economic organizations, which greatly depended on the institutions of the power conglomerate, tried to keep their reserves and opportunities secret, and to present their own interests as those of the branch or the 'national economy'. On the other hand, they were encouraged to do so by the fact that the ambiguities of intraconglomerate power relations appeared to them as uncertainties and contradictions in norms and expectations; moreover, these norms were mostly informal ones, which made the sense of uncertainty and contradiction even greater. Thirdly, the economic organizations, instinctively or consciously sensing the instability of intra-conglomerate power relations, did not dare to attach themselves unequivocally, or to show their cards openly, to any of the conglomerate's institutions. Fourthly, in the total image based on the synthesis of individual bargains, those economic organizations that found themselves in a bargaining position more frequently and were able to assert their interests more forcefully than others—the large firms—were overrepresented, without this becoming sufficiently recognizable. Last, but not the least, by the time an overall image had emerged on the basis of individual bargains, the original interests of the economic organizations could have been modified in the bargaining process in directions that could not have been precisely assessed in advance.

If one studies the method of directly perceiving partial interests as exemplified by economic organizations, it becomes obvious that only the interests of ill-defined 'phantom masses'—including large companies—could be mediated through the channels of the power conglomerate, while the apex of the conglomerate was able to preserve its image of society, based on its own internal logic, which did not clash with its excessively general, vague, and positive self-image.

As the strength of 'phantom masses' is perceived through a synthesis of single bargains, the extremely difficult task of assessing and comparing them is *usually carried out after the event*. László Antal (1985) has called attention to the fact that in order to gain various favors, the economic organizations exercised pressure on the institutions of the power conglomerate in the same direction but independently of one another, with the result that in a large number of those cases the institutions did not register until later that an excessive distribution had taken place. This means that the power conglomerate lacked even the elementary ability either to recognize and take account of a given partial interest if the direct pressure was relatively small, or to control overly strong pressure groups by promoting less vigorous ones.

A more concrete analysis of the operation of the power conglomerate reinforces my earlier statement that *interest inclusion through the institutional channels of the power conglomerate was overwhelmingly coercive, selective, and guided by short-term interests*. I may now add that *as the recognition of the strength of the phantom masses usually occurred after the event, the forced interest inclusion did not necessary have to be a conscious one.*

Therefore, in my opinion, the mechanism of interest integration, in the developed phase of 'existing socialism', was not a mechanism which included interests, but basically a *mechanism in which interests included themselves* and in which the apex of the power conglomerate could occasionally relate to the various societal groups, but never to the totality of the system's interests. *In other words, the system could not be controlled from the bottom, and was incomprehensible from the top.*

The social and economic mechanism in which interests included themselves was extremely unstable due to the peculiarities of the indirect mechanism of economic management. The behavior and interrelationships of its actors were not regulated by any verifiable norms, so that there were no publicly demonstrable institutional safeguards of their integrity and stability. In close connection with this, the actual responsibility of the various actors for the negative socio-economic processes was shrouded in darkness, providing ample opportunities for the creation of scapegoats. The responsibility for various socio-economic problems was not borne, in proportion to their real role, by those who had caused them. Rather, in keeping with the interests of those who happened to be in a dominant position, the blame was laid on the 'weakest link in the chain'—the individual least capable of interest assertion—who was then taken to task. (Hungarian examples were the abolition or merger of industrial branch ministries in the early 1980s and the closure of companies somewhat later [Szalai, 1989b].) The fear of becoming a scapegoat led to increasing efforts towards diluting and blurring responsibility, which made the process cumulative, and this self-reinforcing mechanism was further boosted by growing economic difficulties.

## THE QUASI-AUTARCHIC STRUCTURE

The issue of interest integration was indirectly affected by an important feature of the economic mechanisms under 'existing socialism', called 'quasi-autarchic' and 'quasi-developed' by Ferenc Jánossy (1969). Essentially this meant that from the early 1950s the Soviet leadership, followed by the status groups in power in the different countries of the 'empire', enforced the implementation of an autarchic, self-contained economic policy, even in those small East European countries short of raw materials. The decisive motive was the development of heavy industries in each country, particularly with the rapid establishment of military industries in mind (cold war). Another important factor was the Soviet leadership's intention to prevent the development of a separate ring of integration enjoying at least a relative degree of independence. It was in the power interest of the Soviet leadership that the countries of Eastern Europe should unilaterally depend on its shipments of raw materials, and that in shaping their economic structure they should be neither able nor forced to coordinate their developmental objectives in the spirit of some kind of deliberate division of labor. Consequently, from the 1950s, the economies of East European countries—while emulating the macrostructure of a big and developed economy rich in raw materials and therefore capable of self-sufficiency—became totally exposed to the world economy, at first primarily to the Soviet, then increasingly also to the Western. Thus their basic openness manifested itself as dependency. On the other hand, as the brief first phase of extensive industrialization gave way to the intensive phase, it became clear that an economic structure alien to the conditions of the countries involved could not ensure any efficient new production as the corollary of lasting growth. This is the essence as well as consequence of quasi-autarchy and quasi-development. (Iván Berend T. [2003] noted another important consequence of economic isolation, namely isolation from the processes of technical and technological innovation in the West and the adverse effect of this isolation on lasting and effective growth.) Yet another consequence was the overcentralized structure of big companies mentioned earlier, since the model for the giant firms of the period was supplied by the heavy industries.

## The Constraint

The socio-economic mechanism in which interests included themselves could operate relatively smoothly, based on relatively predictable behavioral rules and bargaining mechanisms, as long as the economy was in a state of relative expansion, above all in the phase of extensive economic development. This was a prerequisite for redirecting resources to the large companies in a dominant position, which were by and large less efficient than average, and to their 'framework', that is, the heavy industries, in such a way that those from whom resources were withdrawn were not shaken to their foundations, in other words, so that they had resources to take away. This system of redistribution, however, necessarily weakened the efficiency of economic operation (Bauer 1982; Szalai 1989b), and therefore after some time all could be satisfied only by *overdistribution*. This, in turn, could be financed only by growing external debt. (By 1987, the countries of the Soviet empire had accumulated a total convertible debt of USD 75 thousand million net, distributed as follows. Poland: USD 35.3 thousand million, Hungary: USD 15.8 thousand million, GDR: USD 10.5 thousand million, Romania: USD 4.8 thousand million, Bulgaria: USD 4.6 thousand million, Czechoslovakia: USD 4.0 thousand million [Salgó, 1989]. In 1989, the gross convertible debt was as follows. Soviet Union: USD 58.5 thousand million, Poland: USD 40.8 thousand million, Hungary: USD 19.2 thousand million, Bulgaria: USD 10.6 thousand million, Czechoslovakia: USD 7.9 thousand million, Romania: USD 0.6 thousand million [Lanigne, 1995].) In countries where the status group in power rejected such debts—most spectacularly in Romania—or tried to avert it with limited success, political repression grew of necessity: the general demand for the constant growth of living standards and the 'underrepresented' partial interests could be suppressed only by means of political dictatorship. The 'methods' of growing debt and political repression were simultaneously applied, for instance, in Poland after the suppression of the Solidarity movement. The problem of the Soviet Union, as the 'center of the empire' and a huge country rich in raw materials, was somewhat different, although the nature and operation of authority (overgrown and disintegrating power centers, the predominance of large companies, and inefficient redistribution) showed similarities to the above description. (I will return to this, and to the Yugoslav problem, later.)

Thus expansion in this system inevitably led to the accumulation of external debt and sooner or later resulted in the breakdown of earlier power relations and behavioral norms.

The spectacular beginning of this process can be dated to the late 1970s (in Hungary, it can be linked to the change of economic policy in 1978 [Szalai, 1989b]). In this period, the first, expansive phase of the socio-economic mechanism, in which interests included themselves based on relatively predictable behavioral rules and bargaining mechanisms, ended in crisis and the restrictive phase began. *However, regarding the entire history of 'existing socialism', this was in fact the beginning of the total crisis of the system.* Although certain elements of reform appeared, and there was even a vaguely worded demand for a comprehensive reform program, the power conglomerates responded to the dramatic recognition of overdistribution with individual and informal restrictive measures that corresponded to the logic of the economic system and were made possible by the constraints of the economic and political power relations. However, these measures further damaged the productivity of the economies. The crisis was not primarily indicated by a radical deterioration of certain quantitative parameters, but rather by the fact that this mode of managing tension did not mitigate but actually enhanced it.

Tamás Bauer (1982) describes this situation as follows:
"In the early 60s (in the countries of the Soviet bloc – E. Sz.), the slowdown was enough to restore the balance of foreign trade and to lessen internal tension. This time the debt of the small countries continued to grow until 1978–1979, while growth slowed down and tensions over the internal supply of raw materials and goods increased. Bulgaria, Czechoslovakia, and Hungary succeeded in halting growing debt only by new radical measures, such as stopping the growth of living standards, radical directives concerning prices and various restrictions on investments. The policy of price rises and restricted investments was also experienced in the Soviet Union; however, here the main symptom of crisis was not price rises, but, as in Romania, the worsening shortage of goods. In Poland, the political crisis of the summer of 1980 was triggered by growing deficiencies in supplies and a consolidation policy similar to that of Hungary and Bulgaria (improving the countries' position in foreign trade by restricting domestic consumption and accumulation). *Thus slowdown was not enough to reduce and mitigate tension; on the contrary, it was accompanied by growing tension in the entire group of countries. It is attributable to this fact that the planned targets for 1981–1985 promised the continuation of slowdown.* (Italics mine, E. Sz.)

Before continuing this train of thought, we must make a detour to distinguish between the concepts of *structural crisis* and *crisis*. The structural crisis of a system is primarily, albeit not exclusively, recognized by the 'experts' or the elite of society, who realize that the methods used earlier for dissolving tension have failed and medicines that were effective till now aggrieve rather than improve the patient's condition. Crisis as such, on the other hand, is the nadir, recognized by society in general, where many other severe and acute social tensions and explosions occur. The patient is gravely ill with a high fever.

The condition of the system as described so far indicates a structural crisis of the institutions and mechanisms of economic interest integration. With the exception of Poland, one cannot speak about a comprehensive social crisis or even its beginnings, as the conflicting interests in society were not articulated and did not collide in public. However, this meant a postponement of the crisis rather than a stability of social relations. As the conflicting social interests could not be articulated due to the lack of an open forum, the counterforces to the negative processes could come into being within society only with great difficulty or not at all, while dissatisfaction with the existing conditions remained diffuse and its direction largely unpredictable. The immune system of society, switched off long since, was unable to regenerate.

In addition, further economic reforms were also removed from the agenda. To quote Tamás Bauer (1982): "politicians are aware that those earlier trends that cannot continue are rooted in the economic mechanism, which must therefore be changed. But, learning from the experiences of the 60s, they are also correctly aware of the limits of changes in economic management imposed by the requirement of keeping the political setup unchanged."

The exhaustion of possibilities hidden in the second economy also indicated a crisis. By the late 1970s and early 1980s, the further expansion of the second economy based on existing norms and strategies hit an objective barrier. According to contemporary surveys, time spent on second jobs could not be further increased, so that any new forms could at most have a restructuring effect. More and more, second jobs allowed only the maintenance of an already achieved standard, and not even that in some strata (Farkas–Pataki, 1984).

In Hungary, the crisis of the system became obvious after the dramatic failure of the attempt to revitalize the economy in 1984–1985, when the country's debt doubled in the next two years. Before that attempt, and after years of systematic economic restriction following the change of economic policy in 1978, the top party leadership, or status group in power, had increased its demands for a more dynamic economy (strongly motivated by reports on the dissatisfaction of the population with the deteriorating living standards). At the same time, the managers of economic units—primarily large companies—put increasing pressure on the state party and party state to restart expansion. The overdistribution that ensued from the mid-1980s—through the political and economic tensions generated by it in conjunction with other factors, to be described later—led first to the weakening of the (never very strong) forces that held the system together and then to the disintegration of the system itself.

However, what is more important than the quantitative parameters of overdistribution is that by this time the system had exhausted its opportunities for change and adaptation. According to my researches, the status group in power had earlier responded to the appearance of the external barrier to growth by 'rearranging' its internal power relations, and thereby modifying the operation of the economic mechanism. During such periods, it was primarily the relationship between the state party and party state, on the one hand, and the big companies, on the other, that underwent radical changes. While the significant deterioration of the external balance in 1978 triggered the restriction of the expansionist objectives of the large company managers, the credit crisis of 1982 resulted in the opposite, repeatedly bringing the interests of large companies to the foreground, and even allowing them to dominate the state party and party state. This seesaw could not work during the post-1985 crisis. Rather, what could be seen was the strengthening of the trends of 1983–1985, that is, the further growth of the opportunities for large companies to realize their interests. In fact, this was an important sign of the exhaustion and closure of the opportunities for change within the status group in power and in the economic system (Szalai, 1989b, 1991).

Thus the socio-economic system 'integrated' by the state party and party state—and the Soviet empire together with it—inevitably disintegrated. To put it briefly, the reason was that the power structure had no political legitimacy, and therefore its legitimacy in a sociological sense—while it lasted—could be ensured only by constantly increasing consumption by the population; however, consumer demands 'encouraged' in this way, after some time, breached the integrative mechanism, given the productivity of the system. (In 1989, in an analysis of societal processes in Hungary, I wrote: "At the time of the 1956 revolution, the old elite experienced the strength of the society, and was subsequently afraid of it for more than thirty years... This fear drove the country into debt." [Szalai, 1989a].) On the other hand, the state party and party state, in order to improve its own operational ability, brought to life some puppets that subsequently started to function as autonomous interest centers, eating away the framework and possibilities of the system with their demands (large companies). Finally, in connection with all this, but put in more general terms, the 'integrator' lost its ability to suppress or merely to control and keep within limits the strong and discrete economic and power interests in the post-Stalinist period almost from the first sign of a loosening of the hard political dictatorship and the first mention of categories of goods (money, market, credit, etc.). In contrast to many social scientists today, I believe (and I have believed since the early 1970s) that no categories of goods can be applied, even for purposes of planning, without bringing to life the market mechanism in a society. (Later I will explain why it would not be desirable either.) In 'existing socialism' the market mechanism was present at least in its elements, but since it was either long denied or at least not recognized in its full significance by those 'on top' (and since the institutions of societal control were not functioning as a consequence of the 'democracy deficit'), ultimately it found its way through uncontrolled and uncontrollable detours, breaking up the system itself together with its 'official' logic. I should add that an unrecognized and therefore uncontrollable market mechanism is very likely to break up any system.

# Chapter 4

# Actors of the Open Crisis

## In the Clutches of World Capitalism

The internal tensions and contradictions that resulted in the disintegration of 'existing socialism' cannot, however, be fully explained by the immanent characteristics of the system. What ultimately decided its failure was the fact that the *fundamental operational mode* of the system, which professed itself socialist, *did not, and could not, differ from the logic of world capitalism.* (The countries of 'existing socialism' had to trade with the countries of 'world capitalism,' and, in addition, the ending of the first, dictatorial Stalinist period necessarily meant, among other things, a cultural opening towards countries outside the 'camp.') The extent to which the system did differ—with the exception of some positive elements mentioned earlier—resulted in grave distortions. To put it more precisely: as the socialist experiment was conducted at the semiperiphery of world capitalism, in countries with weak democratic traditions, the system it brought into being could only produce a far weaker societal output than the welfare capitalisms emerging in response to its challenge. Basically this interrelationship is the reason why I have called 'existing socialism' a semiperipheral socialism.

Nevertheless, 'existing socialism' could more successfully solve those problems that derived from its semiperipheral character, at least in the East-Central European region, than those societies that had begun with similar conditions but then followed the road of capitalist development in their main features (primarily the Latin American countries). In contrast to the latter, 'existing socialism' abolished the oligarchic economy and sharp societal inequalities, and was able to produce better results in industrialization, modernization, and even competitiveness (Arrighi, 1991).

However, unlike world capitalism, 'existing socialism' was unable to offer a truly new alternative which could be viable in the long run. In addition to the internal causes listed earlier (or more exactly, partly manifesting itself in those internal causes), the great vulnerability of the system, resulting from its semiperipheral nature, was the basic reason why its classical period—which followed the first, Stalinist, period—was a period of practically complete disintegration almost from the outset.

As far as the concrete mechanisms and the movement of the societal actors within them are concerned, this has the following implications—concentrating this time on the case of Hungary.

The spiraling debt of the country from the mid-1970s catalyzed the birth and growing influence of a market-focused monetarist branch of reform thinking. This despite the fact that there were signs not only of an economic crisis, but also of a general societal one, as I noted in a paper written in the second half of the 1980s.

The signs of the crisis are shown most tangibly by the chapter headings of Ágnes Losonczi's contemporary book (1989): "The Lack and Importance of Financial Means—Over-burdening, Exhaustion"; "Freedom of Acquisition—and Its Confinement"; "The Status Losers—Economic and Societal Decline"; "Greed and Clinging to the Present"; "Societal Gulfs—Obstacles to Community Building"; "Centralization of Living Communities"; "Material Divisions"; "On the Isolating Effects of Operational Disturbances."

András Lányi (1988) characterizes the societal conditions of the day as follows: "During the past thirty years, state socialism has undergone profound changes. It has gradually incorporated into its system some elements of societal bargaining and competition and of individual initiative, which enabled it to consolidate. However, its solidity was not based on the acceptance of norms suggested from the top, but on the fact that these norms were no longer consistently examined anywhere ... It has been convincingly shown that the uncertainty of the rules of the economy favored an externally directed passive behavior, and at the same time inevitably led to voluntaristic improvisations, or so-called manual controls. Less has been said about the socio-psychological consequences of this situation. If solid points of reference are missing, no strategies that can be consistently followed and no moral principles that confirm them can evolve in any area of life. I am convinced that the loss of balance in the economy hides an intellectual chaos. Our dominant ideas do not point beyond the maintenance of our current practice and its self-justification at all costs; and when it appears that this practice can no longer be maintained, society is at a loss, irritated and perplexed as it views its own growing difficulties. In fact, the latent contradictions did not manifest themselves in the form of open conflict for a long time, because it proved to be more advantageous for all to reach compromises on the quiet instead of articulating and openly representing conflicting interests."

According to Ferenc Erős (1988), the crisis of individual careers and life strategies was also becoming increasingly obvious in this period. "Clinical experience, surveys based on in-depth interviews, literary works, etc. indicate that in Hungary a significant proportion of the people have settled for *survival* at all costs. Today these survival strategies are ending in total failure, and what comes next is some form of self-destruction, often a more or less spectacular suicide. This is particularly conspicuous among the intellectuals (see, for instance, the great 'paradigmatic' suicides), but it is certain that other strata are at least as much affected. One effect of the crisis may be that it confirms these negative life strategies, located as they are between the only alternatives of survival or destruction, to the detriment of the quality and values of life."

In a paper I wrote at that time, I defined the crisis as that of 'lopsided autonomy,' a situation in which freedom rights accruing slowly and in an evolutionary way could not be asserted evenly in the different spheres of the individual's life, so that serious disturbances of identity arose as a result. "The proliferation of the phenomena of social crisis, however, does not meet an *external barrier* similar to that of the economic crisis. Signs of crisis, such as alcoholism, the spread of suicides, the growing number of divorces, the increasing proportion of deaths at an active age, etc., are not—or at least not direct—legitimizing factors in the face of possible bankruptcy and its consequences" (Szalai, 1988).

A further important tendency was the continuous erosion of the economic strength of the Soviet Union, including its armament capability, from the late 1970s and the early 1980s, as was pointed out by János Kis (1982). In Kis's words, the Soviet leaders "are keeping unchanging control of the East European influence zone of their state, although they are no longer able to help it out of its economic troubles. In fact, the Soviet Union itself is in crisis. Its national income is growing at an ever slower pace, the supply of goods to the population has been constantly deteriorating since the mid-1970s, the economy is less and less able to bear the burden of the arms race and other expenses of the state's commitment as a global power. The Soviet interpretation of détente has become untenable. The uneven rhythm of the growth of the different nationalities is increasingly consuming the demographic basis of Russian dominance. The top political elite is ageing, important decisions have been postponed for years, and succession seems to be uncertain. The current Soviet leadership wants only one thing in Eastern Europe: to maintain some order. But their successors will have to decide what to do with their inherited bankruptcy. Their decision will obviously depend on their choice of a way out of the internal crisis of the Soviet Union and its unstable position as a world power. That is, if they really make a choice, rather letting the—more or less favorable—political events trigger each other."

By the middle of the decade, it had become clear that the economic decline of the Soviet Union was providing a broader bargaining position for market-oriented reformers, on the one hand, and more economic and political room for maneuver for the East European countries of the 'empire,' on the other (Kis, 1985). In parallel, the attractiveness of the model of Western consumer society had been continuously growing in the broad strata of the society as a result of the earlier slow reforms within the system, which made the opening towards external markets irreversible and led to the spread of the behavioral patterns of 'lopsided autonomy.' At the same time, as social mobility slowed and social inequalities grew more rapidly, the ideal of community society openly disintegrated. In the unofficial ideology of the system, the ideal of 'community man' was replaced by the no less idealized individual consumer, whose advancement was now endangered primarily by the restrictions on consumption resulting from the growing external imbalance of the economy.

From the late 1970s, the structural crisis outlined above catalyzed the birth and activities of *societal counterelites* that articulated the crisis and sought a way out of it. It was primarily these domestic counterelites, voicing the demand for economic balance, urging a further opening of the market and the external economy, and advocating the emulation of the Western consumer model—above all the technocracy of the late Kádár era (in other words, the new Westernized generation growing up under the shelter of power )—that gained strength as a consequence of the processes described earlier.

At the same time, the birth and activities of these counterelites—as I have already stressed—was by no means an autonomous process that could be interpreted merely within the framework of the nation state, but—particularly from the early 1980s—primarily a consequence of the expectations and pressures of the so-called *international financial and economic superstructure*. (The international financial and economic superstructure is the product of the expansion of economic power over continents and nation states, i.e. globalization, and its agents are the international financial organizations and large multinational global companies, linked as status groups. In creating this concept I have strongly relied on the theories of Held, D. McGrew [1988] and Kamilla Lányi [2001].)

> The role of this 'superstructure' has been growing since the mid-1970s, when a comprehensive neoliberal change began under pressure from international big capital, which wished to cast off the fetters of welfare capitalism. Robert Went (2002) writes about the main cause of this development:
>
> "The post-war economic growth created the material conditions for constantly improving living standards and low unemployment as the foundations of the welfare state, which allowed for a significant increase in social and communal services. On reaching the depressive phase of the long wave of expansion it was no longer possible to ensure almost full employment, enhance social security, increase real wages, or reduce poverty. The main concern of employers was the restoration of a *reduced profit rate* (italics mine, E. Sz.), which called working conditions, living standards and the achievements of the welfare state into question."
>
> The 'international class struggle' was intensified by the economic crisis, with international big capital, intent on eliminating the welfare achievements of capitalism, being represented by the international economic and financial 'super-

structure.' This 'superstructure' was becoming even more interested than before, not only in breaking down the welfare achievements of core capitalism, but also in liquidating the 'collectivist experiments,' that is, 'existing socialism.' It had two reasons for wishing to do so. On the one hand, in relation to its neoliberal transformation, the very existence of a rival social structure imitating communality disturbed it more than it had done earlier. On the other hand—due to the narrower economic motivations of the international big capital represented by it (acquisition of markets, a cheap and well-trained labor force, cheap means of production)—it wished to extend its power over the semiperiphery embodied by 'existing socialism.' This was not necessarily a conscious effort on the part of the 'superstructure.' Rather, in Marx's phrase, they "don't know it but they are doing it." Thus the class struggle affected the societies of 'existing socialism' in this specific form.

In close connection with the factors listed above, the growing strength of the 'superstructure' (the effects of which in Hungary are subtly presented by László Andor [2003]) played a major role in enabling precisely the late Kádárian technocracy and its allies, the democratic opposition and the new reformist intellectuals, to organize themselves as a societal counter-elite. It was no coincidence that earlier we identified the debt crisis as the external barrier: for among all the crisis phenomena, the debt crisis was not only primarily suited by its nature to attract the attention of the 'super-structure' but, to put it more strongly, it was actually that focus of illness to which the 'superstructure' could attach itself. In fact, the debt crisis was primarily brought into the debate by the late Kádárian technocracy. The democratic opposition and the new reformist intellectuals, whose main aim was political democratization rather than the management of the debt crisis, joined the late Kádárian technocracy because the basic condition of overcoming the debt crisis was the full opening towards the West and unlimited expansion of the market, which had proved to be the decisive thesis by the mid-1980s.

> The decisive factor in this process was that by now the leaders of the democratic opposition and the new reformist intellectuals had openly abandoned their earlier Marxist or neo-Marxist identity.
>
> It is astonishing that this transformation and its causes were predicted much earlier by György Bencze and János Kis in their Marxist study quoted above: "There must be changes in the organization of society and in the situation of the working class to ensure that the institutions of power are not strong enough to atomize the working class. As long as such changes cannot be foreseen, Marxism in opposition to the official ideology will be in danger of disappearing or being dissolved in non-Marxist ideologies better suited to the social isolation of nonconformist intellectuals. But at least it will no longer be in danger of continuing to be a parasite of official Marxism."

As we have seen, the organization of the 'working class,' with the exception of Poland, did not take place, and the marginals who had broken away from Marxism, missing societal support, entered an informal but gradually more formalized alliance with the late Kádárian technocracy under the shelter of power in a continued attempt to change (at first by reforming and then by overcoming) the system, which by the early 1980s found itself in open crisis. However, in this casting they were inevitably subordinate to the late Kádárian technocracy (Szalai, 1995).

As both György Földes (no date) and Tamás Krausz (2003) point out, intellectuals and social politicians demanding the democratic reform of socialism were also present in the intellectual life of the crisis period of the 1980s. (It was within that trend that neo-Keynesian and Kaleckian economists, such as Róbert Hoch, Éva Radnóti, Andrea Szegő, György Wiener, and Károly Lóránt, formulated their theses, urging a turn towards the internal market in response to the economic challenge, and analyzing the 'debt trap' at a world-system level. [They further included the North–South problem in the relationship of the core and the periphery, calling attention to the role of the developed countries and the international financial organizations in generating and aggravating the crisis by approaching matters from the angle of the world economic power relations.] Their analysis resulted in the message that there was no point in trying to move towards the core because it would not admit the applicant, and that one should not make a fetish out of the market mechanism, and particularly of the crisis-management capability of private property, as the state could not be eliminated from structural change and modernization. A more important process in the period of Soviet perestroika was the activation of intellectuals who believed in self-management and who saw an opportunity for the 'real' democratization of property and social relations in the disruption of former power relations.)

There are two basic reasons why the intellectual advocates of democratic socialism could not be the catalysts of effective societal forces. On the one hand, the 'superstructure,' and its domestic 'favorite' within the power structure—the late Kádárian technocracy—naturally did not, and could not, support the intellectuals' objectives. On the other hand, the intellectuals—in contrast to the democratic opposition—neither distanced themselves from nor openly confronted the status group in power. That (among other things) was why they were unable to marshal broad societal forces behind them.

## Disintegration

Turning to the collapse of the Soviet empire and its causes—including the role of the 'superstructure'—one recognizes two parallel but intertwined processes from the early 1980s.

On the one hand, it became obvious to the Soviet leadership that it was unable simultaneously to perform three 'tasks' set by the 'superstructure': to offer a lifeline to the East-Central European countries slipping into a deeper and deeper debt crisis, and thus prevent their political 'erosion'; to keep pace with the escalating arms race; and to maintain the internal living standards, political stability, and investment capacity of the country.

The East-Central European countries' perception of this situation was described by András Köves (2003) as follows: "The increasing dynamic disadvantages of trade with the Soviet Union united with the decreasing static advantages, and the more the makers of domestic economic policy and the managements of many companies oriented to the Soviet market tried to gain static advantages by maintaining or reinforcing the existing structure, the more pressing the problems and the more severe the dynamic disadvantages became. The crisis of the Soviet economy was obvious; the Soviet ability to deliver and to pay was decreasing."

In addition—or, more precisely, in close connection—acute socio-political tensions developed in East-Central European countries (Szelényi, I., Szelényi, B., 1994), first in Poland (where the working class revolted against its rulers) and then in Hungary (where the societal counterelites became highly active [Szalai, 1991]).

On the other hand (as mentioned in part before), a technocracy and an economic elite, which may be called late state socialist and which were oriented to the West and the market, came into being under the shelter of power, not only in Hungary but in all the other countries of the region, and most of all in the Soviet Union. This development—the intensity of which significantly differed in the different countries—was the result of the behavioral pattern, and in some cases the direct pressure, of the 'superstructure' (Krausz, 2003; Hanley–Matějů–Vlachová–Krejči, 1998).

> Iván Szelényi and Balázs Szelényi (1994) see the fundamental reason for the emergence of rival elites inside the 'communist' elite in that the 'communist' elite failed to bring up its own successors, not wishing even its own children to make a 'nomenclatura' career. I rather believe that those 'children' refused to be 'brought up' in keeping with their parents' taste. Their teens and young adulthood coincided with the beginning of the disintegration of 'existing socialism,' the opening towards the West, and the appearance and spread of Western behavioral patterns and consumer models in the countries concerned, and it was in consequence of those processes that the 'children' resolutely revolted against their parents (Szalai, 1990, 1999).

Under the combined influence of the factors listed above, from the mid-1980s the "Soviet leadership let go of the reins" (in Márton Tardos's phrase), and by the late 1980s, seismic changes were taking place in the entire region, including the 'center of the empire': 'mediated' by the local counterelites, the transformation of the political system had begun.

Western literature on transitology tends to explain the beginning of political system changes by the overwhelming pressure of civic movements (see, for instance, Timothy Garton Ash, 1990). I believe that (with the exception of Poland) 'existing socialism' could give birth only to civic movements of limited strength and the decisive battle was waged not between civil societies and the 'communist nomenclatura,' but between two factions of the power conglomerate, the old 'nomenclatura' and the late state socialist technocracies. (This battle is well portrayed by Bozóki, 1991; Kis, 1997; in the case of Bozóki 2000, 2003 [although his conclusions in the latter work partly differ from my own].) This tendency was strengthened by the fact that from the beginnings of political change (after conflicts of different intensity in the different countries) the late state socialist technocracies had allowed the weak germs of parties to grow out of the weak civil society very fast towards the forums of power, rather than letting them move down, towards society (Szalai, 1989b; G. A. Bryant–Mokrzycki, 1994).

During this period, the intellectual supporters of democratic socialism were more exercised by the question why society did not resist the political changes, which could ultimately lead to the dismantling of 'communal' ownership. (Experiences of 'participant observation.') According to Péter Szigeti (2003), the decisive reason for the lack of resistance was that society did not really regard the system of 'existing socialism' and the so-called 'communal' ownership relations as its own; it did not believe that the property that was soon to be 'privatized' was *its* property. And, as I explained earlier, it had every reason to feel that way.

Ultimately, as far as the major issues of the unfolding change of the system were concerned, the *society* basically remained passive and, with *by and large positive expectations from change*, did not express any doubts even concerning the foreseeable privatization. (Demands for the creation of at least partially direct employee ownership were not [and could not be] decisive [Szalai, 1994].) In addition to the 'democratic deficit' of 'existing socialism' and the strong attraction of the Western consumer model, the sociocultural traditions also played a major role. (This will be discussed in greater detail in the next chapter.)

The changes in the political system were soon followed by the beginnings of changes in the economic system. The primary beneficiaries of this process, which lasted about ten years in the societies concerned, were basically none but the late state socialist technocracy and economic elite (Granville, 2000, Szalai, 2001, Krausz, 2003).

Here only a brief reference can be made to the Yugoslav case. Although Yugoslavia was not an integral part of the Soviet empire and the Yugoslav attempt at self-governance presented a specific, strongly democratic, alternative to socialism, the crisis and open failure of that 'model' coincided roughly in time with the crisis and disintegration of the Soviet empire (if only as a result of the general loss of opportunities and the mood of crisis within the 'socialist camp'). The crisis of the attempt at self-governance—which for many years was also one of the chief sources of the positive hopes of the Hungarian reformers—was caused mainly by the bureaucratic restrictions and the related failure to create a real ownership interest among workers, in addition to the effects of the world capitalist framework and the pressure exercised by the debt crisis of the 'superstructure,' as was established by József Juhász (2001).

China, Cuba, North Korea, and Vietnam are 'holding out' to this day. In my view, the reasons for this are found in the specific historical development, the cultural traditions, the economic starting conditions and, primarily, the hard political dictatorship of the one-party status group in power in these countries. (However, in the limited space available, I cannot discuss these still 'existing socialisms' here.)

Chapter 5

# The Socio-Cultural Heritage and Its Structural Effects

The fact that 'existing socialism' was not, and could not be, either a 'community society' or 'democratic socialism,' and therefore became susceptible to the expectations of the 'superstructure' at an early stage, is due to historically determined socio-cultural factors as well as structural ones.

## The Organic Nature of Inorganic Development

There are no significant historical traditions of community and democratic behavior in the region, including Hungary, and the existing historical traditions are mediated precisely through socio-cultural effects of the opposite kind. The communal, democratic aspirations and revolutions of the Hungarian people were always suppressed, so that they never had an opportunity to carry out a successful collective drive for autonomy. Consequently—as mentioned before—the communities that nevertheless emerged could only be compliant communities with limited functions or highly restrictive communities forced on individuals from above. Our major socio-cultural heritage is the dominance of individual, informal, and atomized interest assertion and the servility related to this.

At the same time, this servility has been the most important feature of the continuously inherited behavioral pattern of the elites leading the society. In his analysis of this feature, István Bibó (1948) writes about the disastrous historical split in the personality types of the elites:

> "Two things are needed for community leadership and guidance, as for any creation: a practical realism bearing in mind what can actually be achieved and an ability to see what matters resulting from knowing the internal rules of the tasks. If a community is driven into the blind alley of some lie, the first consequence is that it cannot find any realistic people capable of seeing what matters, whom it can trust to lead it. It may find any number of practically-minded people, to whom practical work or the possibility of advancement is most important and who are therefore prepared to be 'realists' in the sense that they accept the prevailing lie as reality. Thus their realism is exhausted in supporting and strengthening a basically false structure, shunting it to and fro among the false

existing possibilities. On the other hand, people blessed with the gift of seeing what matters seek a different form of expression, retreat into narrower and smaller communities, or feel increasingly isolated, sulk, take offence, develop eccentric attitudes or become fierce prophets; and it is the eccentrics and fierce prophets who are suited to say what matters."

What matters most in the construct Bibó calls false and untruthful is the compulsion to maintain the semblance of autonomy under conditions of total exposure. This leads to the split within the roles of the elites 'guiding' society (and within societal roles in general). However, this is not merely a Hungarian phenomenon. In our region it is most vividly and tangibly illustrated by literature, the writings of Dostoevsky, Chekhov, Turgenev, Kafka, Musil, Kundera, Kertész, and Grotowski.

It was the socio-cultural heritage outlined above that, on the one hand, expressed and, on the other hand, historically continuously confirmed the decisive feature of the structural development of Hungarian society and of the semiperiphery elsewhere in the region: there had never been either the opportunity or the time for the dominant forms of the organization of the economy and society to be brought forth from within the society by an organic development. Therefore the dominant forms of economic and social organization in these countries, with the cooperation of the falsely realistic elites engaged in coerced adaptation, had always been created by power from above and from outside (see primarily Erdei [1976] and Szűcs [1983]). Paradoxically, however, this inorganic development had an 'organic' character, and it was precisely this 'inorganic organic' character that marked the emergence and structure of 'existing socialism' and subsequently played a decisive role in its downfall. In Hungary neither the factory councils set up after 1945 nor the workers' councils formed in the 1956 revolution could survive and take root (being either integrated into the power structure or violently liquidated). Despite these spontaneous democratic efforts, the structure of the economy and society continued to follow the dominant central (and Soviet) model of heavy industry and large companies.

Analyzing the historical traditions of Hungary, András Lányi (1988) writes:
"For centuries our history unfolded within the framework of alien states. More recently we have twice obtained autonomous statehood together with a bill for historical crimes, presented in the form of dictates after military collapse. But the other condition, identification with the existing political institutions as our own, which is even more important than our relationship to their genesis, is also missing. This condition is the accumulation of positive social experience gained by supervising and influencing the institutions, which could be called the democratic element of social identity. In contrast, our experience is dominated by exposure and subordination to state bodies that dominate our

historical experience. These bodies, motivated by imperial or class interests, have been able to maximize their centralizing efforts thanks to the inability of civil society to resist them and to their own excessive force supported from outside. Their power and their right to interfere has extended to every area of life and continues to do so to this date.

For centuries, decisions affecting the entire society had been made far from society at the apex of power shrouded in mystery. 'Common issues' did not mean issues that we should have settled communally, but rather issues (such as foreign affairs, finance, defense) that were too important to be influenced by public opinion. In keeping with the historical traditions of the region, the theoretically communal society was built by the state appropriating the right to dispose over all the means of societal reproduction without actually taking the organization of the state itself into public ownership. Moreover, even if some organs for controlling and counterbalancing the state were developed by civil society, they eventually withered away or were integrated into the omnipotent state structure, which operated beyond the influence of the citizens. This process gradually eliminated the institutional and mental preconditions of a subsequent decentralization and socialization."

Gáspár Miklós Tamás (2001) concisely described the past and the present as follows:

"Modernization in Hungary (quite a rare process in the region) took place in three waves (1867: the Compromise, mutual co-optation of the bourgeoisie and the aristocracy, curbs on the Catholic state-church; 1945/49: agrarian reform, coercion by terror, industrialization, accelerating equality through mobility, broad general education, creation of a stratum of intellectual cadres, forced mobilization, mixture of surveillance and censorship, methodical dictatorship; 1988/89: democratic and capitalist system change, reduced popular participation, repeated attempts at autocratic rule [reform fascism] as class rule, passivity, constant legitimacy crisis, stability deriving from impotence, vigorous but one-sided economic development). As I recently tried to point out, all this took place under the protection of external powers (Austria, the Soviet Union, the West or 'Europe') through the structures of a benevolent, Western-oriented, paternalist, and cosmopolitan comprador elite, without involving, and probably against the wish of, mistrustful Hungarian citizens, who paid for it three times by abandoning their national independence and self-reliance."

Therefore it can also be explained by historical conditioning that the societies concerned kept largely quiet at the time of political system changes around 1989, expecting a fundamental improvement of their situation from the counterelites emerging from 'existing socialism,' whom they trusted almost blindly for a short while, before they turned away with their trust fading. Thus societies involved were pushed from 'state socialism' to new capitalism not by spontaneous social movements coming from below, but by elites with a significant personal continuity, who in the majority of cases sooner or later replaced their earlier links to state socialism with a dependency on international big capital (the 'superstructure') in the process.

## SEMIFEUDAL TRADITIONS

Adopting a different approach, but in close connection with what has been shown before, we find that in 'existing socialism' and its subsequent disintegration some important elements of semifeudal social relations were reincarnated. Although the master–servant relationship disappeared almost at a stroke, servility (mixed with secret contempt), respect for authority, the dominance of informal interest assertion, and a 'transfer' of responsibility for the solution of life's problems to the cloudy regions of power (with a simultaneous mistrust of power) all indicated the survival of feudal traditions.

Generalizing the problem, one may say that the 'inorganic organic nature' of societal development outlined above derived not only from the external exposure of the region but also from the survival of internal, semifeudal traditions, which reinforced its propensity to depend on 'external powers,' while the external exposure in turn continuously reproduced the semifeudal behavioral patterns, attitudes, and values. More specifically, the semifeudal attitudes inherited by 'existing socialism' facilitated the lasting 'occupation' of the region by the Soviet Union, and at the same time, the strong external dependency further stabilized the semifeudal motivations and relationships. (All the more so, as the society represented by the 'occupiers' preserved its own semifeudal character.) This heritage in its turn inevitably manifested itself in the passivity of the society and the disintegration of 'existing socialism.'

## A DUAL SOCIETAL STRUCTURE

Studying in more concrete terms the socio-cultural traditions inherited by 'existing socialism,' it was the specific survival of the dual societal structure of the interwar period in Hungary, described by Ferenc Erdei (1976), in the dichotomy of the economy and culture of the first society, and of the economy and culture of the second society. László Laki (1991) writes:

> Based on the available data, I believe that the condition of Hungarian society in the 70s and 80s, described by researchers as a 'duplication' of society, economy, and values, etc.—as in 'first' and 'second' economy—cannot be derived exclusively from the socialist conditions that had become dominant after World War II. It can be historically proven that societal, economic, and other 'duplications' had already existed prior to it, and that such an interpretation of the

problems appeared in contemporary literature as well. Consequently, to me, the problem is not why and how the economy and society were 'duplicated' under socialist conditions, but what happened to the inherited 'duplication' under those conditions...

One should deal separately with the—in my view, rather simplistic—approach which regards the 'first' economy as exclusively 'bureaucratic' and 'redistributive' and the 'second' as being an operation or process of the 'market.' I see the matter as something more complex, not only because both spheres were dominated by a chaotic mix of 'market' and 'bureaucratic' transactions, but also because it is an oversimplification to present the 'second' economy as if it had been dominated by developed commodity and monetary relations. This does not correspond to the reality, for it is now known that the most extensive sector of the domestic 'second' economy was linked to subsistence production (agriculture) and is characterized by natural transactions and the enormous proportion of self-supply within them even today.

Based on Laki's idea, we ultimately see that in the Hungarian variant of 'existing socialism,' the earlier, even spatial, duality was transformed into an *inner duality,* or the relative autonomy analyzed above, of the various societal cells, such as the organizations of redistribution, companies, and even individuals. It was in this particular way that the dual structure 'defended' and 'preserved' itself, only to reappear, in overtly separate societal structures, in the new system that has emerged by now (Szalai, 2001).

Chapter 6

# The One-Party System and the Transitory Society

## One-Party System and Power Relations

According to Péter Szigeti (2003), "in any transitory society the dominance of a system of public ownership could be ensured only if the power was exercised by a de facto one-party system... The one-party system was the safeguard of public ownership."

In this part of my book, I will try to prove that the ownership relations of 'existing socialism' were not those of public ownership. However, it is true that, for the reasons listed earlier, semiperipheral socialism could be maintained, if at all, only by a one-party system. At the same time, I am of the opinion that a one-party system can by its nature only be the expression and corroboration of authoritarian or dictatorial power, as is conclusively proved by the history of 'existing socialism.' Therefore I do not believe that the "dialectical democracy" recommended by Szigeti—that is, a reformed one-party system—could be a relevant solution of the problems of democratically managed public property. If a society has the opportunity to assert its interests and will only through a complex, multiple-tier decision-making mechanism with *one* sole apex, the authoritarian or dictatorial power structure can be taken for granted, no matter how wide-ranging the safeguards incorporated into the system may be. Sooner or later the apex will inevitably begin to function as an autonomous 'interest center,' which is why it is necessary for the society to choose between 'alternative apexes,' in other words, for the apexes to be *directly replaceable*. But that is already a multiparty system (which the workers' councils of 1956 regarded as eminently compatible with the self-management of their factories).

I am of course aware of the grave internal problems of a parliamentary democracy based on the multiparty system and, as I have written elsewhere (Szalai, 2003), it is clear to me that this system has been thrown into a grave crisis by the present world of globalization and is struggling against a serious 'democratic deficit'—but only as a system linked to the nation state. I am convinced that one of the main slogans of the international alter-globalization movements—that the global challenge must be met by a global response and that international big capital and its logic must (or can only) be controlled or rolled back through global institutions—can be realized only by creating and operating *international* institutions built on the principles of multiparty parliamentary democracy (which would by no means reduce the importance of local institutions and direct democracy).

## THE TRANSITORY STAGE

Péter Szigeti, following the line of scientific socialism, describes 'existing socialism' as a transitory society. Once again I agree with him up to a point. 'Existing socialism' was truly a transitory society; however, it was not moving towards 'developed socialism,' or communism, but towards new capitalism.

I have already spoken of the complex nature of 'existing socialism' with regard to its societal and, primarily, political and economic power relations. I have also mentioned that this complexity eventually became the source of the system's disintegration. In order to shed light on the transitoriness resulting from the complexity, I had to review its entire history. But now I must also discuss in some detail the main features of the new system that came into existence with the disintegration of 'existing socialism' (even if I do not analyze every aspect of it here). This should widen our horizons and deepen our generalizations.

I start with the thesis that in 'existing socialism' both the life situations of the individuals and the communities bore the marks of transitoriness.

Earlier I characterized the *life situations of individuals* as a relative autonomy, which contained the contradictory elements of a strong pressure and demand for adjustment accompanied by estrangement, increasing liberation and individualization. In the new capitalism, which has replaced 'existing socialism,' the relative autonomy of the individuals constituting the majority of society is being eliminated. The pressure and demand for adjustment becomes even stronger and now manifests itself as exposure, while the process of individualization ends in atomization—in other words, the estrangement becomes total. Where once there were frames of reference, which made this phenomenon *stand out*, they are now disappearing. This means that since even the compliant or enforced communities are disintegrating, the individuals are losing all the bearings they need to retain or develop their individuality. In fact, without some kind of community no individuality can take shape and sooner or later the identity which is the basis of individuality—and freedom—is eliminated (Szalai, 2003a).

Looking at this process from the angle of *communities* what we see is that they too were transitory in 'existing socialism.' In the 'warmth' of the compliant or enforced communities, there could be merciless, albeit often camouflaged, assertion of individual interests and ruthless rivalry.

> György Spiró (1981) masterfully characterizes the relationships within the system in a spectacular episode of his novel *Az ikszek* (The Xes). One of the protagonists conducts a profound and tearful psychological conversation with

another character. Both are deeply moved. Then the first leaves and reports the second to the authorities.

János Kenedi (1996) on a broad empirical basis presents the secret police network of the Kádár system, which penetrated even the smallest societal groups. The informer, who was often 'trapped' through financial and career inducements, was often linked to his or her victims by real and deep emotions. (This was the experience of several victims acting as 'participant observers.')

Tamás Almási's documentary film *Kitüntetetten* (Decorated, 2001) features a socialist brigade consisting mainly of women, which is created from above, but which develops into a real community. Their lives show genuine solidarity, communal responsibility, and cultural improvement (through images of mutual support, committed social work, and compulsory but sincere reading of literature) side by side with the authoritarian power relations of the Kádár system and the underhand private schemes based on these (as in the case of the brigade leader who drafts the workers under his command into building his own dacha in their spare time).

At the same time, it should be stressed (not least on the basis of the above examples) that although these communities were rare and usually artificially created for limited functions, in the settled and consolidated period of the system they were often able to fulfill real community tasks. A movement of this kind was the Young Communist League of the 1960s and 1970s, which offered real community experience to broad strata of young people and, for all its limitations, provided an opportunity for the discussion of the 'great' societal issues. Similarly, the institutions of public accountability in the workplace, albeit within strict boundaries, made the internal power and interest relations (including, for example, remuneration) relatively transparent and capable of being influenced, at least to some extent, by the workers.

The presence of mosaic-like communities alongside the surviving traditional societal patterns may be explained by the fact that, although the organization and operation of communities was rather hindered or at least restricted by the status group in power and by smaller or bigger 'bosses,' the advocacy of communalism by the official ideology of the system had set in motion the creation of certain standards and values. On the other hand, given 'human nature,' even in the compliant or enforced communities group dynamics could produce a process leading to the development of internal solidarity, at least of a limited kind.

I must hasten to add that in these circumstances the development of communities was of a peculiar nature. Since the groups, in the majority of cases, were not based on free decisions and voluntary commitments and their members were not really free, autonomous individuals, they were overly hierarchical and authoritarian, with a rigid allocation of roles. At the same time, they were inclined to become exclusive and inward-looking, and even to develop a strongly erotic atmosphere, known also from artistic reproductions. One may even say that the internal structure and external relationships of the smaller and larger communities of 'existing socialism' reflected on a small scale the peculiarities of the macrostructure of the society. The effects of the semifeudal socio-cultural heritage also appeared in communalism.

On arrival at new capitalism both opposites were eliminated: on the one hand, in the larger part of society even those rare communities with limited functions disintegrated (or were transformed into occasional, short-term interest alliances); on the other hand, the opportunities for individual interest assertion were largely restricted, and controlled competition was replaced by the open dominance of the somewhat stronger over the somewhat weaker. The rules and norms of whatever competition still existed became totally incomprehensible to the majority of society. (In the workplace, the institutions of public accountability were almost completely abolished [remuneration became entirely secret], and employees felt that they had far less influence over decisions than in the 'old' system [Bruszt-Simon, 1992]. Although in the initial years, the citizens still had positive expectations from competition within the political institutions, by the mid-1990s they no longer believed that these offered them a real say in political decisions [Andorka, 1996]. The Czech writer Jiří Kratochvíl, in his novel *Truchlivý bůh* (Sad God, 2003), describes in dark colors how a family, whose members used to support each other in representing their common interests in the 'outside world' under 'existing socialism,' became a mafia in the new capitalism.)

Individuality and communalism, limited as they were in 'existing socialism,' were eliminated in the new capitalism. What emerged was a society consisting largely of exposed atoms concentrated, if at all, into short-term interest alliances—a society woven through by a dense web of subordination and superordination, which at best restricts competition.

What caused this change? Did the complex nature of the societal relations in 'existing socialism' mean that it was transitory by itself? My answer is negative. A complex society is transformed into a transitory one only if several factors exercise a joint effect. However, one must distinguish between predisposition and fundamental reasons.

Predisposition was present, firstly, in the complexity of societal relations, which was not consciously recognized and publicly engaged with. As we have seen, the unrecognized element in 'existing socialism' that surfaced with irresistible force was the market as both a value and a mechanism.

Predisposition, secondly, was present in the unbalanced nature of the complexity, in other words, the dominance of one element (or group of elements) over the rest. In 'existing socialism' forced adjustment or required adjustment and the competition deriving from narrow individual aspirations were *much stronger* than either the pursuit of real individuality (freedom) or the desire to create a community. Consequently civil society was weak, with the result that the macrosocietal power relations began to change as they did, and once they had changed, the transformation outlined above occurred almost at a stroke.

## Summary of societal transformation

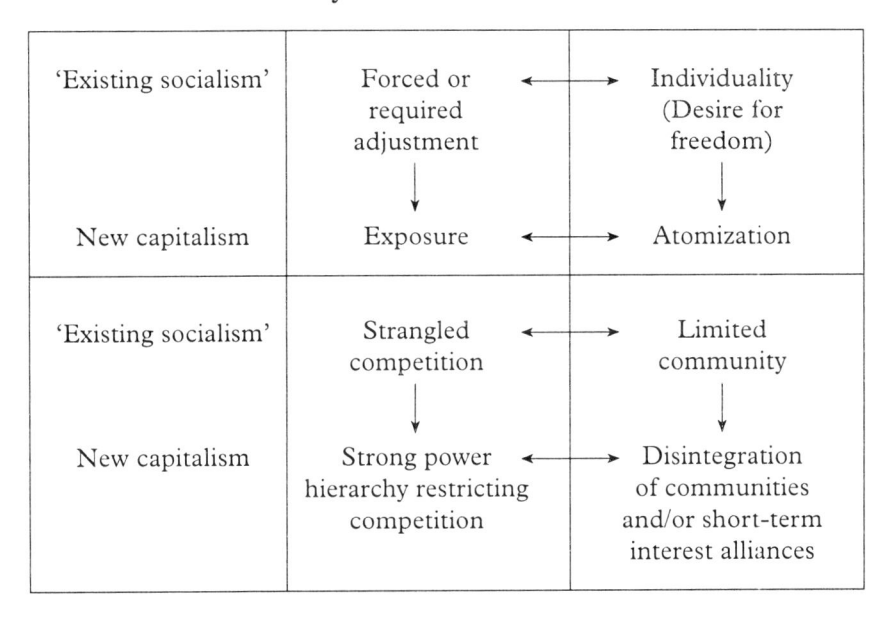

| 'Existing socialism' | Forced or required adjustment ⟷ | Individuality (Desire for freedom) |
|---|---|---|
| New capitalism | ↓<br>Exposure ⟷ | ↓<br>Atomization |
| 'Existing socialism' | Strangled competition ⟷ | Limited community |
| New capitalism | ↓<br>Strong power hierarchy restricting competition ⟷ | ↓<br>Disintegration of communities and/or short-term interest alliances |

The fundamental reason for the transformation can be found in the changes in 'macropower' relations. I will explain this by a—substantially modified—summary of Bourdieu's (1983) theory of capital. (For the main principles and details of the transformation, see Szalai [2001].)

When the status groups in power began to build 'existing socialism,' they had only political capital, which they gradually converted into cultural and economic capital. (One may also say that they turned their original power as status groups into a power with class traits by the inclusion of new actors.) A decisive change took place when they failed to transfer this capital to their 'descendants' in an unchanging structure and with the same value content. Therefore the cultural capital of the successors of the 'communist nomenclatura,' the late state-socialist technocracies (and their intellectual allies), was no longer defined by their 'parents' but, against the background of the unfolding economic crisis, by an external power, the international economic and financial 'superstructure.' One part of the 'communist nomenclatura' was unable, and another part unwilling, to prevent the late state-socialist technocracies (and their intellectual allies) converting this cultural capital, which was fundamentally different from their own, into economic, and subsequently political, capital. As a result, a vigorous modification of the economic and political capital itself began with the change of generations within the status groups in power (in keeping with the interests and demands of the 'superstructure'), and the process ended in the changes of the political system.

In the initial phase of their ascendancy, the late state-socialist technocracies had a certain interest in strengthening individualization and communalism, which helped to dismantle the 'macropower' relations of the complex system. However, the situation changed fundamentally once they had reached the apex of political power and, together with their allies, began to convert their political capital into economic capital by launching privatization. A 'genuine redistribution of capital and income' began under the leadership of the late state-socialist technocracies, as a result of which ownership was transferred from the majorities of the societies concerned to the minorities, and in particular to the new economic elites (Szalai, 2001). However, this process could take place, and its benefits institutionalized for the 'winners,' only at the cost of the fundamental disruption of the lives and organizations of the majorities. The new economic elites were not interested in the further development of individuality and communalism, but, on the contrary, in their total liquidation (Szalai, 2003b). On the principle of "they do not know it, but are doing it," by keeping the social actors in uncertainty (both in and outside the workplace), they, with the assistance of the media (and the support of the 'superstructure,') or more precisely the mechanism that came increasingly under their control, were the prime cause of the complex process of transformation described above. That, above all, is how and why complexity had become transitoriness.

At the same time, it was not inevitable that the intervention of an external power, the 'superstructure' in this case, should have 'magically' transformed complexity into transitoriness. It could (and was bound to) perform that 'magic' because it enjoyed a significant superiority of power, because it was for its part moving from complexity towards one-sidedness (the new liberalism) and finally because in connection with its own problems it had a strong interest in eliminating the complexity of the societies exposed to it.

According to the intentions of its power elites, it was the historical function of 'existing socialism' to destroy—or in reality, to loosen up—the semifeudal conditions it had found (of which the bourgeois–democratic conditions probably would not have been capable under the given historical circumstances), and to create the socio-structural and cultural prerequisites of semiperipheral linkages with—or more precisely, reintegration into—the system of world capitalism. In other words, 'existing socialism' was to generate an industrial workforce and subsequently—after a period of "dictatorship of modernization," analogous to the original accumulation of capital (which varied in depth and time scale in the various countries)—to create "life worlds," marked by relative autonomy and the interplay of communalism and competition, resembling those of the classical period of welfare capitalism (albeit with significantly different internal proportions and conditions that can be regarded as a mixture of the semifeudal heritage and elements pointing towards capitalism). Last but not least, 'existing socialism' was to bring forth elite groups governing a semiperipheral integration into the system of world capitalism, and, in parallel, to depoliticize and demobilize society.

The road ran as follows: semifeudal, semiperipheral capitalism; → semiperipheral socialism; → semiperipheral new capitalism. In other words, 'existing socialism' created—and could create—only the conditions for preserving our starting positions of the interwar period.

## ALTERNATIVES

Although 'existing socialism' had several models, as shown by my reflections so far, even in retrospect, I cannot see how the system as a whole could have developed very differently from the way it did. (As we saw, the tendencies that might have pointed towards a 'real' socialism, particularly in the impenetrable force field of the countertrends, proved to be extremely weak.) On the other hand, I believe that there were some real alternatives to the new capitalism emerging from socialism. I hasten to add: within the 'world logic' of capitalism. A fundamentally different system—as in the dawn of 'existing socialism'—could have been created and run exclusively by political dictatorship (and a foreign policy of total isolation).

In fact, a different kind of capitalism could have been 'made.' On the one hand, there were in the region, including Hungary, traces of initiatives and efforts coming from below to enable at least a group of employees to obtain a share of the so-called state property destined to be dismantled by privatization. This would have made it possible to introduce elementary forms of worker self-governance, at least at the level existing in English-speaking countries (Szalai, 1994)—all the more so since, counter to the assumptions of neoliberal economists, worker ownership, at least as occasionally realized in Hungary, operated no less effectively than classical private or state ownership (Boda–Neumann, 2002). These 'germs of self-management' daily prove their viability even in an environment dominated by capitalism. On the other hand, it would have been possible, and necessary, to avoid the present situation, in which the high 'globalization level' and the high proportion of processing industries in the countries of 'existing socialism' hide a range of assembling activities that could be provided anywhere else at any time in the world market (Pitti, 2002; Szalai, 2003a). As a result, the comparative advantage of a well-trained and educated but relatively cheap labor force is allowed to go to waste. (In Hungary, today it is more or less a thing of the past.)

There could have been basically three, interrelated, ways of avoiding the omissions and traps described above. First, during the second half of the 1980s or at the time of the changes to the political systems at the latest, the important social counterelite groups – that is, the democratic oppositions that came into being within the 'existing socialisms' – rather than merely speaking about a 'social market economy' in general, should have formulated some clearly-defined ideas about the social and economic structure of the 'social market economy' towards which the countries should be directed. This would have been possible if the democratic oppositions had developed in the direction of a fundamentally social-democratic identity (in keeping with their earlier ideological traditions) in the critical one or two years of political change at the latest. It was not to be. The majority of the democratic dissidents soon shed their leftist mantle accompanied by ideas of self-management, and setting out towards liberalism many of them arrived directly at neoliberalism and conservative liberalism (Szalai, 1995).

Second, from the mid-1980s, or at the time of the political changes at the latest, the intellectual advocates of democratic socialism, mentioned earlier, should have openly confronted and parted company with the status group in power. At the time of the political changes (and only then), they would have had a moral opportunity to mobilize the 'working class.' Rather than defending to the last ditch the 'achievements' of 'existing socialism' (to which I myself have given credit in the past), they should have developed a public strategy whereby the 'working class' could not only defend itself but also resolutely assert its interests in the neocapitalist system.

This too was not to be. The democratic dissidents and the advocates of democratic socialism jointly could have represented a sufficiently strong counterbalance to the late state-socialist technocracies (and other old and new economic elites). Although in the circumstances a complete neutralization of these actors of power would have been a hopeless (and unnecessary) enterprise, the possibility of controlling and restraining them was not ruled out from the outset. The lack of control resulted in a significant superiority of the late state-socialist technocracies, and these (together with other groups of the economic elite) not only prevented a somewhat broader expansion of employee ownership, but in their neoliberal zeal also proved to be totally unable to generate a coherent vision of a societal and economic structure and a related concept of economic policy. Moreover, they were eager to impede all the serious societal forces that tried to do so. (Thus they placed the extreme right at the advantage of being able to take up this theme and thereby promote its popularity.)

Last but not least: the East-Central European countries breaking away from the Soviet empire should have restricted the sharp competition that broke out between them from the first moment of political change, and adjusted their strategies and tactics for bargaining with the West. It is not true that the 'system-changing' countries had no bargaining position. As mentioned above, they had excellent cheap labor, jointly represented a significant demand market, and possessed at least partly valuable means of production.

Thus, given a different evolution of the components listed above, there could have been an alternative to the 'existing capitalism' of the region, which combines all the disadvantages of capitalism without any of its real advantages (Szalai, 2001; 2003a; 2003c). A more organic (and possibly lengthier) process of transformation, better adjusted to the proclivity of individuals and groups for renewal and change, could have taken place, and as a result, perhaps a more balanced social structure, with fewer inequalities and less injustice, could have been born out of this labor.

CHAPTER 7

# The Message

Although the greatest socialist experiment so far has failed, the challenge that had created it has not lost its validity, even for those paths that ultimately branch off from it. Indeed today, in the age of new capitalism, the 'temptation' to reflect on the societal problems that constitute that challenge has become stronger than ever before. The question is whether a harmonious realization of the values of liberty, equality, and fraternity can be ensured, given the concentration of the means of production and other kinds of property, and the tendency towards their further concentration.

Today it is not possible to begin to formulate a response to that challenge without a summary of the problems, errors, and even crimes resulting from the ideologies, attitudes, and behavior which represented the foundations and driving forces of 'existing socialism.'

I would like to summarize the lessons (perhaps not quite objectively) as follows. There are no exceptional people (despite "We communists are special people") who have the right to impose a model invented in the study on other people—no one can be made happy against his or her will. There are no exceptional people who need not be controlled by others, because uncontrolled power inevitably runs wild and lends itself to abuses. The idea of a perfect society is an illusion, and a dangerous one at that: the idea of the perfect society is in fact the omelette for which any number of eggs is supposed to be worth breaking (Berlin, 1996). Societies built on a single principle and a single value inevitably lead to dictatorships, because the assertion of other principles and values can be restricted only by violence. But these principles and values, sooner or later, will find ways of blowing the society apart. This also holds true for the market and market values, because there will always be scarce goods that can be efficiently distributed only by the market. Therefore, the complete elimination of the market in any more equitable society of the future is also an illusion. Likewise, the idea of a society free of conflict is an illusion; there is (and there must be) constant struggle between the different societal forces and values, because they can find their balance in the long run in no other way. There are no ultimate 'solutions' and it would not be good if there were any. The condition of perfect equality and solidarity can never be reached, because man is only a "moderately altruistic creature" (Rawls, 1997; Kis, 1998) and the values of equality and solidarity can only be approximated. Without a chain of voluntarily created and accepted microcommunities bringing together free individuals, even the idea of a society merely approximating communalism will remain an eternal illusion. Only the results of organic development nurtured from below are enduring, because the inherited socio-cultural patterns bind people even where the societal conditions change radically, since such changes occur or can be brought about only very slowly.

In my understanding this is the message in the bottle. I could not have written one word of this book if I did not believe in a society with more solidarity, more justice, fewer inequalities, and (as a result) more freedom than the present one—in short, socialism.

CHAPTER 8

# The Chances of the New Socialist Alternative

This is not the place to expound my thoughts about the possibilities and main principles of a socialism of the future in their totality. As I have written extensively about these elsewhere (Szalai, 2003a) I will only give a sketch of the issues I consider most important.

## THE NEW LEFTIST APPROACH

In assessing the chances of a socialist alternative, the most important task is to map the existing or emergent *organic processes* that may prepare the overcoming of capitalism in the longer run. I am emphatically speaking about organic processes that come into being from within capitalism, and not about how any kind of socialist movement could grasp power. As was shown by Adamovsky, it is precisely this way of thinking that is the essence of a new leftism. According to Adamovsky, the Leninists and the social democrats had one thing in common—they believed that they had to acquire control over the state before they could begin to reform the society from above. In fact, as we have seen, there are some problems with this attitude. "For power is not located in the national states alone, but disseminated throughout society (including our minds). Moreover, it is not very much constrained by national boundaries. In other words, if we 'storm the Winter Palace' today, we would not 'have the power' as a result, but only a nice empty building." Adamovsky also reminds us that when the great leftist movements of the past seized power, they became similar to the power structures they had struggled against. They "tended to reinforce the people's passivity and/or authoritarian practices, instead of contributing to liberate and empower all of them equally. Power is not a 'neutral' tool that you simply use for any purpose (whether good of evil), but always an unfair and oppressive type of relationship" (Grubacic–Adamovsky, 2003).

## THE CRISIS OF CAPITALISM

The most important processes pointing *also* towards the organic socialist alternative arising from capitalism feed on the general crisis of the capitalist system itself. This crisis began with the disruption, and deepened with the liquidation and self-destruction, of the rival Soviet empire. Together with the removal of every barrier to the logic of capital asserting itself, the corrective mechanisms of the system, which had been indispensable earlier, were also switched off. (The latter affects primarily the institutes of multiparty parliamentary democracies. While in the classical age of capitalism political pluralism and political rotation were perhaps the most important safeguards of bourgeois democracy, they are now becoming tools for manipulating public opinion as part of the drive to divide the forces opposed to global international big capital. Thus the competition of political parties linked to the greatly weakened national institutions can no longer be a competition of real alternatives.) But this means that the internal contradictions of capitalism are already breaking through the surface with elemental force. That is the essence of new capitalism.

Seen from a broader historical perspective, the general crisis of capitalism began already with the struggle for the economic redistribution of the world by World War I. Subsequently, in response to fascism and then 'existing socialism', the corrective mechanisms restraining the logic of capital came into action, culminating in the birth of the West European welfare states. As far as the current crisis is concerned, we know that any counterpowers that have or may come into being at the periphery or semiperiphery of the world economy and thus are unable to produce an autonomous operational logic of their own—for example, the Islamic community—can only delay the victory of the logic of capital over the forces restraining it. For the same reason, they can only delay the intensification and breakthrough of the contradictions created by the logic of capital within itself and leading to its own crisis.

The current crisis of capitalism and the internal contradictions embodied in this crisis have several symptoms. In what follows, I will list them in a rather sketchy fashion. At the same time, I will pay special attention to those elements that may point towards a new socialist alternative.

## An Important Theory and Its Critique

Wallerstein (2000) indicates three trends *within* the logic of capital that restrict the general rule of the mobility of capitalism, i.e. the unlimited accumulation of capital: "the triple pressure is tending to make unfeasible the primary motor of the system and hence is creating a structural crisis." The first trend is the *real wage* level as a percentage of production costs, calculated as an average throughout the world economy. "Obviously, the lower this is, the higher the profit level, and vice versa." The level of real wages is determined by the power relations between employers and employees. The principal mechanism by which capitalists worldwide have been able to limit the political pressure of employees for increases in their real wages has been the relocation of certain sectors of production to other zones of the world economy where lower average wages prevailed. "Such a mode of conducting the class struggle is dependent on there always being new areas of the world-system into which to relocate, and this is dependent on the existence of a significant rural sector that is not yet engaged in the wage labor market. But the latter is precisely what has been diminishing as a secular trend. The deruralization of the world is on a fast upward curve. It has grown continuously over 500 years but most dramatically since 1945. It is quite possible to foresee that it will have largely disappeared in another 25 years. Once the whole world-system is deruralized, the only option for capitalists is to pursue the class struggles where they are presently located. And here the odds are against them."

The second trend "disturbing to capitalists" is the cost of disposing of *hazardous wastes*. The solution of this problem is similar to relocation as a solution to wage costs. "It works as long as there are previously unutilized areas in which to dump waste." But such areas are inevitably becoming more scarce, with the logical consequence that sooner or later all the costs will be "internalized." This puts further pressure on the profits of the various companies.

The third pressure on the profit rate is *taxation*. According to Wallerstein, there have been constantly growing demands from the public sphere, resulting in "steadily rising tax rates in virtually every country, with at most occasional, slight reductions. But of course, at a certain point, such redistributive taxation reaches levels where it interferes seriously with the possibility of accumulating capital."

In my view, the burdens on the profit rate are more complicated than Wallerstein sees them. To put it bluntly, I find the essential factors that disrupt the capitalist system from within somewhere else.

As far as the conditions for keeping down the proportion of the real wage are concerned, these can be manipulated by the economic elites. One of the most important features of the present crisis is the *growth of overproduction*, which paradoxically hits the capitalists and at the same time gives them the opportunity to secure lasting and constantly increasing reserves of unemployed labor to be used for the purpose of holding those still employed at bay. This is possible because capacities not fully utilized or surplus products remaining in stock do less damage to the rate of profit than the possible increase of wage costs, on the one hand, and the reduction of the price of goods, on the other. This is the fundamental reason for the vigorous growth of inequalities all over the world and, as pointed out by Thurow (1996) among others, for the fact that more and more people and even countries become redundant and are not even regarded as subjects of exploitation.

In the long run this process may truly undermine the position of the economic elites. (Ildikó Ékes [2003] calls attention to the growing role of the hidden and black economy in ensuring the purchasing power necessary in our age. "In that area, production is still capable of employing a large number of people, indeed a growing workforce, because tax evasion is spreading. Thus, for the time being, it absorbs at least part of the workforce squeezed out of the visible economy. This provides them with income, and purchasing power is created even for goods produced in the visible economy.")

The previous logic may be continued in relation to the admission of hazardous wastes. Areas divested of practically any kind of economic activity may, for a long time ahead, view this 'enterprise' as their only source of income. The practice of 'externalising' harmful wastes may not reach its limits until these wastes accumulate to such an extent and become so toxic that they can no longer be separated from the core countries and prevented from affecting them even across distant continents.

Finally, as far as the strength of social pressure for constantly increasing taxes is concerned, my opinion again differs from Wallerstein's. Currently the economic elite is able to fend off this pressure very successfully, as global capital is moved to and fro in the world economy practically without being taxed. Here a constraint may emerge, as it already is doing at the semi-peripheries, in that the (deliberate) dismantling of the public sphere may sooner or later deprive capital of a properly trained, physically and mentally well-maintained workforce (Szalai, 2003c). Thus the devaluation of human capital may fundamentally undermine the ideology of the much-quoted knowledge society.

## Medium-term Alternatives

To sum up: the real constraint on capital accumulation may be the worsening shortage of purchasing power, ecological crisis, and the erosion of human capital. However, some socio-political constraints may emerge even before a fatal collision with these. In that case three scenarios are possible. The first is the further strengthening and advance of fundamentalist movements, starting partly in the Third World (primarily the growing force of the militant wing of the Islamic movement), and partly in the cores (see the growth of xenophobia and anti-Semitism in Europe). The second is the open dictatorship of the global international economic elite (indicated by the entire current policy of the United States [primarily on the advice of 'business circles'] and the Iraq war).

It is of crucial importance that those two scenarios may even become two 'subprocesses', mutually reinforcing each other, of one and the same process (which they have indeed already become to some extent). In that case a war (or wars) threatening the very existence of humanity would be inevitable in the long run. Therefore the third scenario cannot be anything but the new socialist alternative. This would be the emergence of a society which at least limits the uninhibited assertion of the logic of capital and carries in itself such structural specificities and safeguards as may, in constant struggle for a balance, represent or produce a pluralism of liberty, equality, and fraternity.

## "Networking" and Its Consequences

Before assessing the chances of these three scenarios, a brief survey of the technological and structural changes of the market during the past decades, together with their influence on the world of labor and the related changes in the nature of ownership relations, is called for.

According to Pine (1993), fundamental technological changes have taken place in the world during the past decades, modifying the behavior of the market actors. The adoption of information technology by the economy is not characterized by long-term commitments of investment, but by rapid change. Consequently, production based on information technology does not tolerate any lasting commitment, or at least radically reduces its terrain. The production units are loosely linked in changing networks that may easily disintegrate.

On the other hand, the majority of those employed in current information technologies *are completely out of touch with the physical processes.* A decreasing proportion of labor is directly linked to material processes, and its larger part is used in the intellectual preparation of production, services surrounding production, and contacts with consumers. This kind of work is easy to outsource; it is eminently suited for *transferring the employees to tele-work only loosely linked to the company,* as opposed to the traditional kinds of work on the production line. The industrial revolution in its time concentrated workers in noisy and smelly large factories, taking them away from their homes and sharply separating working hours from leisure. Now the exact opposite of that historical process is in progress.

According to Katalin Szabó (2003), tele-work is only one variant of so-called *conditional employment.* (Some further variants are labor on loan, part-time employment, etc.) Employees belonging to this circle have two things in common: the *temporary, uncertain* nature of their employment, and the *loose linkage* to the company that employs them. "This form of course continuously questions the status of the workforce involved. The ground under their feet is constantly shaking; their work and services are set in a context of continuous competition. This, in itself is nothing new, for the constant changes of production and working conditions are corollaries of the market economy. The uncertainty of jobs and unemployment are the basic structural characteristics of this economic system." But the degree and extent of the uncertainty, compared to the middle third of the 20th century, represents a surprising novelty.

It is an important finding of Szabó that the close and logical connection between the technological and production trends and the changes experienced in the world of labor is not a new phenomenon. At the dawn of the industrial revolution, when the system of factories emerged in the wake of capital concentration, the workforce also had to be concentrated. When capital standardized production by breaking it up into simple phases and organizing it along the production line, labor was also standardized. When a high degree of specific capital, that is, equipment used exclusively for one particular production process in the giant factories, became characteristic, the commitment of the workforce was also upgraded and, given that practice could be acquired only in long years spent on a specific process, the workforce also became more or less 'fixed in concrete.'

Today, as always ever since its birth, capitalism is trying to force its employees into a production and technological system that is efficient from its own point of view. Szabó writes: "If production is globalized, the workforce must also become 'employable without boundaries.' If production is flexible, working conditions cannot be fixed for years, much less for decades. If production is variable, or modular, the workforce must also become modular, and be ready for the most diverse kinds of employment, with a diversity of competencies in its portfolio."

The revolutionary changes outlined above, which may be called revolutionary, have some very important societal consequences—but these may develop in a very different, indeed opposite, direction.

According to Castells (2002), the basic consequence of networking is the emergence of a dual world in which everybody increasingly becomes individualized and follows his or her personal inclinations and interests, while the communities also gain in strength as everybody seeks personalities similar to his or her own in order to establish a network and build sociable, cultural, or business communities with them. In fact Castells' vision is nothing but a move towards a new socialist alternative, but the processes outlined may take this direction only where some very clearly defined conditions exist or come into existence.

Currently it seems as if processes running counter to real individualization and to the strengthening of communities are taking place. We are witnessing a weakening of macro- and microcommunities as a result of *excessive* individualization, on the one hand, and a growing uncertainty of status, on the other, which endanger the boundaries of the ego, individuality itself. Without real communities, as mentioned above, identity as the basic prerequisite of individuality cannot develop or withers away. (Some consumption sociologists engaged in the apology of new capitalism welcome that as a positive development. In their view, the disintegration of our identity into roles played at various points of the 'network' is in reality a liberation from our own tyranny over ourselves and from the tyranny of society over us. We can no longer be 'conscripted' by any authority, because we do not even exist in reality. The real struggle for freedom is the elimination of the ego, an escape into, and hiding behind, roles offered by the 'network' and the related consumer society.) Therefore, we may speak about atomization, the disintegration of societies, rather than real individualization. The enlarged choice of consumer goods and the message of the media under the rule of the economic elites create merely the semblance of the latter. Estrangement becomes total as *the previous standards are reduced to ashes.*

There is a great danger of this process spreading and leading to two others.

On the one hand, the second scenario, the open dictatorship of the economic elite, may be realized. It may be accompanied by the open restriction of consumer 'freedom,' the renewal of Fordist traditions in employment and the open elimination of civic rights. Its ideology may be religious—as manifested by some trends in the United States—and its socio-psychological foundations may be the product of the elemental force of an atomizing society's demand for community.

On the other hand, that demand may make the first scenario a reality, triggering not only the advance of religious ideas and values, but also that of aggressive, authoritarian fundamentalisms, which would endanger the most basic values of enlightenment.

The last possibility is an accelerating development towards the ultimate limits of capital accumulation, mentioned above, ending in collision with a disastrous lack of demand, ecological crisis, and the degradation of human capital.

We are at a crossroads, and *at present we still have* a free choice. It would seem that the only positive 'way out' is the socialist alternative. Two interrelated factors point in this direction. One is the emergence and growth of the international alter-globalization movements and the motivation of young people participating in them. The other is the growing value of 'knowledge goods' and 'emotional goods.' The increasing diversity and complexity of knowledge and of the human relations accompanying networking may result in the degradation of 'real,' profound, knowledge and emotional relations, but it may equally well result in the opposite, in their actual enrichment and enhancement—particularly if there is a significant social demand for this.

My hopes, in broad agreement with Ágnes and Gábor Kapitány (1995), lie in the latter process, which is already taking place in many separate instances. They are based on the fact that knowledge and emotions are 'goods' which in the long run cannot be appropriated, owned, or marketed without being worn down and destroyed, but which are enriched when they are shared. Therefore I hope that the growing prominence of the 'goods' of knowledge and emotion will limit and/or significantly modify the processes of appropriation and the operation of market mechanisms prevailing today. (According to Rifkin [2000], private ownership is weakening and new forms of ownership are gaining strength in the economy today. Some interesting ownership structures—neither private nor communal, but somewhere between the two—are emerging. In an increasing number of sectors in the economy of the core countries there is a new phenomenon that Rifkin calls 'access' ownership, because its 'object' is owned by none but can be used—or 'accessed'—by anybody who observes the rules.)

## THE SIGNIFICANCE OF ALTER-GLOBALIZATION MOVEMENTS

Two questions emerge in relation to what has just been said. The first question is whether those with the knowledge and emotion would be prepared in the long run to formulate and represent the interests and concerns of those who do not possess these 'goods' or possess them only in a limited degree, and whose ability to assert their interests is weak. In fact, there appears to be a tendency for the emergence of a 'knowledge and emotional elite' which continues to have the possibility to function on the basis of traditional values and principles, and which tries—and may, at least in the short run, be able—to monopolize the knowledge and emotional 'goods.' (This can be clearly observed in the structure of the present multinational companies: at the apex there is the highly qualified elite operating the traditional decision-making mechanisms [based on direct, face to face relations] and immediately below it, the mass of the "conditionally employed" kept in an exposed position [Szalavetz, 2003].)

The second question is whether the organic processes outlined would be strong enough to fulfill those positive expectations, or whether the 'ruling elites,' in keeping with their customs, would transform the benefits of those processes into parts of the consumer culture offered by them.

My answer is a complex one.

The alter-globalist movements arise from within new capitalism as an attempted answer to its contradictions and crisis. Their main source is the 'overproduction' of young graduates and intellectuals in the core countries. Most of their members are young people who have not been absorbed by the labor market as a result of the general crisis of overproduction. (This is one of the reasons why the 'system' has extended the time spent by students at university. The long years of study are becoming less and less an investment for an adulthood spent at work, and more and more a way of life, an organic part of the consumer culture of the young.) However, increasing numbers of these young people do not want to be integrated; on the contrary, they show a growing aversion to the career paths and 'adult' ways of life offered by the new capitalist societies. They do not wish to turn their knowledge and human relations into market goods, and they resolutely demand values associated with community. It is these young people who constitute the most significant base of the international alter-globalization movements.

Albrow (1997) describes these new movements—which he calls 'globalist' rather than 'antiglobalist'—as follows: "Globalist movements derive their strength from the freely given commitment and surplus energy of ordinary people worldwide. They have no significant stock of capital in the form of equipment or money. What they have is human, or more precisely, cultural, capital. They gain from value commitments, knowledge, and information which are commanded neither by the state nor by employers nor by coercive religion, and which do not have to be devoted by individuals to domestic consumption." Those 'values' include the representation of the cause of the poor peoples of the Third World, resistance to the growing general inequalities, environmental pollution and war, as well as seeking out and demonstrating the behavioral patterns of direct democracy.

The alter-globalization movements are organized with the help of the most modern means of communication, which enables them to confront the 'networks of capital' with their own networks.

It is highly significant that the movement has been spreading from the core countries. As we have seen, one of the most important lessons of 'existing socialism' was that only the behavioral patterns encountered in the core countries can become a truly attractive mobilizing force for the whole world. Therefore, so long as the 'owners' of knowledge and emotion in the core countries preserve their fundamental interest in the 'saleability' of their goods, there is hope that the movement will maintain a lasting solidarity with the exploited and excluded, be they in the core countries or on the peripheries and semiperipheries.

According to Adamovsky, the new left, which is the leading force of the antiglobalization movements, decisively differs from the old left in that it *"seems to be more interested in undermining power than in accumulating it"* (italics mine, E. Sz.). Its aim is "to build and expand autonomy, that is, our capacity to live according to our own rules" (Grubacic–Adamovsky, 2003).

But was this not the basic aim and ideology of the student revolts of 1968? We know that it was. And we can see that the majority of the leaders of the rebels of those days now occupy important positions at the control desks of new capitalism or have risen to be sulking postmodern professors.

There is a chance to repeat history. At present, one of the prime organizational principles of the alter-globalization movements is consciously to avoid the creation of power centers, to operate decision-making mechanisms based on consensus and—last but not least—to keep clear of political parties. At the same time, efforts are also being made to direct the movement into the sphere of traditional politics and a hierarchical order (naturally, with the slogan of making alter-globalization activities more effective). By all previous experience, this could lead directly to the dismantling of the movement and its integration into the system of new capitalism.

However, I think that this scenario may be avoided, because the 'global situation', the 'situation' of capitalism today, is fundamentally different from that in 1968. As I have attempted to show, in contrast to the late 1960s, after the fall of 'existing socialism' those forces that exerted both internal and external pressure on capitalism, but at the same time, acting as self-correcting mechanisms, helped to regenerate it—forces that would be capable of integrating in their self-movement the aims of the rebelling young generations' desire for a fundamentally new and different society—are no longer present. For the sake of the survival of humanity, a global counterforce committed to the triple value system of liberty, equality, and fraternity must be marshaled against global capital, a task for which the alter-globalization movements are primarily predestined by their position and orientation.

I am aware that, owing to the limits of my knowledge and foresight, I have said very little about the concrete system of 'new socialism.' However, I am sure that that system cannot be produced by any single act, or even a series of acts. If the new socialism is to come into existence, it will be the result of organic processes, in which the behavioral patterns of autonomy, communality, and solidarity presented by the alter-globalization movements will have far greater significance than their concrete political demands and actions.

Perhaps there is still a possibility of avoiding a situation in which a universal tragedy would shock humanity into realizing the need for a new societal order.

\*

To me, those are the major issues of the future, or rather of the foreseeable medium term, which should be kept on the agenda by the left continuously and without fail. Considering the shorter term—that is, the next five or six years—we should focus our attention on the struggle of the two models of capitalism, the Anglo-Saxon neoliberal and the European welfare model. (In this context Howard [2002], Maull [2002], and Owen [2003] are worth reading.) We should do so all the more because the lasting defeat of the European welfare system in this struggle—or the abandonment of its achievements in competition with the neoliberal 'logic'—would not only further strengthen inequalities and injustice (in the world, in our region, and in our own country) in the short run, but might also harm our long-term prospects and the cause of socialism.

# Bibliography

ALBROW, MARTIN. *The Global Age. State and Society Beyond Modernity*. California, Stanford: Stanford University Press, 1997.
ANDOR, LÁSZLÓ. "A láthatatlan kéz, avagy: miért kevésbé rossz Magyarországon az IMF reputációja, mint külföldön?" (The Invisible Hand, or: Why Is the Reputation of the IMF Less Bad in Hungary Than Abroad?) *Egyenlítő* vol. I, no. 2 (July 2003): 50–54.
ANDORKA, RUDOLF. "Elégedetlenség" (Dissatisfaction). (Working Papers of the Hungarian Household Panel 7.) *Társadalmi páternoszter 1992–1995*. eds.: Sík, Endre and Tóth, István György. Budapest, 1996 January.
ANTAL, LÁSZLÓ. *Gazdaságirányítási és pénzügyi rendszerünk a reform útján* [Our Economic Management and Financial System on the Road to Reform]. Budapest: Közgazdasági és Jogi Könyvkiadó, 1985.
ARRIGHI, GIOVANNI. "A fejlődés illúziója. A félperiféria koncepciójának megújítása." (The Illusion of Development. A Renewal of the Concept of the Semiperiphery). *Eszmélet* nos. 15–16 (1991): 145–180. (Originally published in: Marx Centanno 6., 1991).
ASH, TIMOTHY GARTON. *The Magic Lantern. The Revolution as Witnessed in Warsaw, Budapest, Berlin and Prague*. New York: Random House, 1990.
BAUER, TAMÁS. "A vállalatok ellentmondásos helyzete a magyar gazdasági mechanizmusban" (The Contradictory Situation of Companies in the Hungarian Economic Mechanism). *Közgazdasági Szemle* no. 6 (1975): 115–132.
———. "A második gazdasági reform és a tulajdonviszonyok" (The Second Economic Reform and Ownership Relations). *Mozgó Világ* no. 11 (1982): 3–25.
BENCE, GYÖRGY – KIS, JÁNOS (M. RAKOVSKI). "A szovjet típusú társadalom marxista szemmel" (The Soviet-Type Society Viewed with Marxist Eyes). *Párizsi Magyar Füzetek*, (1983).
BEREND, T. IVÁN. "Kompország az EU-kikötő előtt" (A Ferryboat Country at the EU Port). *Népszabadság* (5 April, 2003): 21.
BERLIN, ISAIAH. "Az emberiség göcsörtös fája. Fejezetek az eszmék történetéből" (The Crooked Timber of Humanity: Chapters in the History of Ideas). Edited by Henry Hardy. Budapest: Európa Könyvkiadó, 1996. (Originally published in J. Murray, London, 1990).
BIBÓ, ISTVÁN. "Eltorzult magyar alkat, zsákutcás magyar történelem" (Distorted Hungarian Frame, Blind Alley of Hungarian History). (1948) In: Bibó, István: *Válogatott tanulmányok, 1945–1949*. (Selected Papers, 1945–1949.) (Budapest: Magvető Könyvkiadó, 1986), pp. 569–620.
BIHARI, MIHÁLY. "Politikai rendszer és szocialista demokrácia" (Political System and Socialist Democracy). ELTE Faculty of Law and Political Science, Department of Scientific Socialism, 1985.

BODA, DOROTTYA – NEUMANN, LÁSZLÓ. "A munkavállalói tulajdon visszaszorulása Magyarországon" (The Retreat of Employee Ownership in Hungary). *Közgazdasági Szemle*, no. 2 (2002): 143–157.

BOURDIEU, PIERRE. "The Forms of Capital." In: John G. Richardson: *Handbook of Theory and Research for Sociology of Education*. New York, (No publisher) 1983.

———. "Gazdasági tőke, kulturális tőke, társadalmi tőke" (Economic Capital, Cultural Capital, Societal Capital). *A társadalmi rétegződés komponensei. Válogatott tanulmányok* (The Components of Social Stratification. Selected Papers). Edited by Angelusz, Róbert (Budapest: Új Mandátum Kiadó, n.d.), p. 156–177.

BOZÓKI, ANDRÁS. "A magyar átmenet összehasonlító nézőpontból" (The Hungarian Transition from a Comparative Point of View). *Valóság* no. 8 (1991): 23–41.

———, ed. "Alkotmányos forradalom" (Constitutional Revolution). Bozóki et. al. *A rendszerváltás forgatókönyve: Kerekasztal-tárgyalások 1989-ben*. (The Scenario of the system Change: Roundtable Talks in 1989). vol. 7. Budapest: Új Mandátum, 2000.

———. *Politikai pluralizmus Magyarországon* [Political Pluralism in Hungary]. Budapest: Századvég Kiadó, 2003.

BRYANT, G. A. CHRISTOPHER – MOKRZYCKI, EDMUND, eds. *The New Great Transformation? Change and Continuity in East-Central Europe*. London and New York: Routledge, 1994.

BRUSZT, LÁSZLÓ. *A politikai intézményrendszer reformja és az érdekképviseletek szerepe* [The Reform of the Political Institutions and the Role of the Organs of Interest Representation]. Manuscript. Budapest, 1987.

BRUSZT, LÁSZLÓ – SIMON, JÁNOS. "The Great Transformation in Hungary and Eastern Europe. (Flying Blind)" *Yearbook of the Hungarian Political Science Association*, (1992): 77–203.

BUNCE, V. "The Political Economy of the Brezhnev Era: The Rise and Fall of Corporatism." *British Journal of Political Science* 13 (January 1983): 129–158.

———. "Domestic Reform and International Change: Gorbachev in Historical Perspective." *International Organization* 47. 1. (Winter 1993): 107–138.

CASTELLS, MANUEL. *Cities and Social Theory*. Edited by Ida Susser. Oxford: Blackwell Publisher Ltd, 2002.

CLIFF, TONY. *State Capitalism in Russia*. London: Pluto Press, 1974.

COLLINS, RANDALL. "Prediction in Macrosociology: The Case of the Soviet Collapse." *American Journal of Sociology* 100, no. 6 (May 1995): 1552–1593.

CSANÁDI, MÁRIA. "A döntési mechanizmus szerkezete" (The Structure of the Decision-making Mechanism). *Társadalomkutatás*, no. 4 (1987): 2–15.

———. *Honnan tovább? A pártállam és az átalakulás* [On From Where? The Party State and Transformation]. Budapest: T-Twins Kiadó, MTA Közgazdaságtudományi Intézet, 1995.

DJILAS, M. *The New Class. An Analysis of the Communist System*. New York: Praeger, 1957.

———. *The Unperfect Society Beyond the New Class*. London: Methuen, 1969.

ÉKES, ILDIKÓ. "A tudásalapú társadalom paradoxonai" (The Paradoxes of the Knowledge Society). *Munkaügyi Szemle* (May 2003): 13–15.

ERDEI, FERENC. "A magyar társadalom a két világháború között. I–II" ( Hungarian Society between the Two World Wars. I–II). *Valóság* nos. 4–5., 23–53, and 36–58 (1976).

ERŐS, FERENC. "Válság és pszichológia" (Crisis and Psychology). *Arat a magyar*. (Harvesting Hungarians). A Szociálpolitikai Értesítő és a Fejlődés-tanulmányok sorozat különszáma. Institute of Sociology, HAS, 1988.

———. *A válság szociálpszichológiája* [The Social Psychology of Crisis]. Budapest: T-Twins Kiadó, 1993.
FARKAS, KATALIN – PATAKI, JUDIT. "Nyolc esztendő mérlege" (The Balance of Eight Years). *Jel-kép* no. 1 (1984): 10–18.
FEHÉR, FERENC – HELLER, ÁGNES – MÁRKUS, GYÖRGY. *Diktatúra a szükségletek felett* [Dictatorship over Needs]. Budapest: Cserépfalvi Kiadó, 1991.
FERGE, ZSUZSA. *Társadalmunk rétegződése* [The Stratification of Our Society]. Budapest: Közgazdasági és Jogi Könyvkiadó, 1969.
FÖLDES, GYÖRGY. *Az eladósodás politikatörténete (1957–1989)* [The Political History of Growing Debt (1957–1989)]. Budapest: Institute of Political History, n.d.
GÁBOR, R. ISTVÁN. *A „második" gazdaság* [The "Second" Economy]. Budapest: Közgazdasági és Jogi Könyvkiadó, 1981.
GERSCHENKRON, ALEXANDER. *A gazdasági elmaradottság történelmi távlatból* [Economic Backwardness in a Historical Perspective]. Budapest: Gondolat, 1984.
GOMBÁR, CSABA. "Politika—címszavakban" (Politics—by Catchwords). *Politikatudományi Füzetek* 1. Budapest: ELTE Faculty of Law and Political Science, Department of Scientific Socialism, 1983.
GOSTA ESPING-ANDERSEN. *Social Foundations of Postindustrial Economies*. Oxford: Oxford University Press, 1999.
———. *The Three Worlds of Welfare Capitalism*. Oxford: Blackwell Publishers, n.d.
GRANVILLE, JOHANNA. "The Metamorphosis of the Russian 'Cleptocracy' and the Global Extension of Russian Organized Crime." *Contemporary Politics* 8, no. 4 (2000): 343–349.
GROSSMAN, GREGORY. "The Party as Manager and Entrepreneur." *Entrerpreneurship in Imperial Russia and the Soviet Union*. Edited by Gregory Guroff and Fred V. Carstensen. New Jersey, Princeton: Princeton University Press, 1992.
GRUBACIC, ANDREJ – ADAMOVSKY, EZEQUIEL. "Global Movement: Interviewing Adamovsky." (2003). *http://www.zmag.org/sustainers/content/2003-06/19grubacic-adamovsky.cfm*
HABERMAS, JÜRGEN. "A kommunikatív cselekvés elmélete" (The Theory of Communicative Action). Special issue of *Filozófiai Figyelő* and *Szociológiai Figyelő*. Budapest: ELTE, n.d.
HANKISS, ELEMÉR. *Közösségek válsága és hiánya. Társadalmi csapdák. Diagnózisok* [The Crisis and Lack of Communities. Societal Traps. Diagnoses]. Budapest: Magvető Kiadó, 1983.
———. "Második társadalom." (The Second Society). *Valóság* no. 11 (1984): 2–16.
HANLEY, ERIC – MATĚJŮ, PETR – VLACHOVÁ, KLÁRA – KREJČI, JINDŘICH. "The Making of Post-Communist Elites in Eastern Europe." Working Paper of Research Project "Social Trends" 4/1988. (1998). In: *http://archiv.soc.cas.cz/stwp/98-4.doc*
HEGEDŰS, ANDRÁS. "Adalékok a tulajdonviszonyok szociológiai elemzéséhez" (Contributions to the Sociological Analysis of Ownership Relations). no. 6 (1969): 1134–1139.
HELD, D. MCGREW. "The End of the Old Order? Globalization and the Prospect for World Order." *Review of International Studies* 24 (December 1998): 219–243.
HOFFMANN, STANLEY. "Világkormányzat: utópia helyett" (World Governance: In Lieu of Utopia.) *2000* vol. 15, nos. 7–8 (2003): 9–16.
HOUGH, JERRY F. – FAINSOD, MERLE. *How the Soviet Union is Governed*. Cambridge, MA. and London: Harvard University Press, 1979.
HOWARD, DICK. "The Last Agenda After September 11. An American View." *Internationale Politik und Gesellschaft. International Politics and Society* 4. (2002): 68–83.

JÁNOSSY, FERENC. "Gazdaságunk mai ellentmondásainak eredete és felszámolásuk útja" (The Origin of the Present Contradictions of Our Economy and the Way to Eliminate Them). *Közgazdasági Szemle* nos. 7-8 (1969): 115-132.

JENKINS, ROBERT M. "Two Models of Economic Integration in Hungary: Consequences for Careers." EERS. vol. 4, no. 3 (1990): 557-579.

JUHÁSZ, JÓZSEF. "A jugoszláv önigazgatási modell" (The Yugoslav Model of Self-Management). *Múltunk* nos. 2-3 (Special issue of Papers on the History of Socialism.) (2001): 276-293.

KAPITÁNY, ÁGNES – KAPITÁNY, GÁBOR. "A szellemi termelési módról" (On the Intellectual Mode of Production). *Eszmélet* no. 28 (1995): 147-161.

KEMÉNY, ISTVÁN. "A magyar munkásság rétegződése" (The Stratification of Hungarian Workers). *Szociológia* no. 2 (1972): 36-48.

KENEDI, JÁNOS. *Kis állambiztonsági olvasókönyv I.-II.* [A Small Reader of State Security I-II]. Budapest: Magvető, 1996.

KIS, JÁNOS. "Gondolatok a közeljövőről" (Thoughts on the Near Future). *Beszélő* no. 3. Compound Edition, Budapest, (1982): 115-124.

———. "Korlátainkról és lehetőségeinkről." (On Our Constraints and Possibilities). Monori Tanácskozás jegyzőkönyve (Minutes of the Monor Conference), Manuscript, 1985.

———. "Reform és forradalom közt. I–II" (Between Reform and Revolution. I–II). *Kritika* no. 6 (1997): 32-41, no. 7 (1997): 30-42.

———. "Az igazságosság elmélete: John Rawls magyarul" (A Theory of Justice: John Rawls in Hungarian). *Világosság* 39, nos. 8-9 (1998): 36-66.

KLIGMAN, GAIL. "Reclaiming the Public: A Reflection on Creating Civil Society in Romania." *East European Politics and Society* 4, no. 3 (1990): 393-438.

KONRÁD, GYÖRGY – SZELÉNYI, IVÁN. *Az értelmiség útja az osztályhatalomhoz* [The Intellectuals' Road to Class Power]. Budapest: Gondolat Kiadó, 1989.

KORNAI, JÁNOS. *A szocialista rendszer. Kritikai politikai gazdaságtan* [The Socialist System. A Critical Political Economy]. Budapest: Heti Világgazdaság Kiadó Rt., 1993.

KÖVES, ANDRÁS. "A KGST-kereskedelemtől az EU csatlakozásig (A kereskedelmi reorientáció néhány főbb kérdése a rendszerváltó országokban, különös tekintettel Magyarországra). I–II." (From CMEA Trade to Accession to the Union. Some Major Issues of Commercial Reorientation in Countries Engaged in System Change, with Special Reference to Hungary. I–II). *Közgazdasági Szemle* nos. 7-8 (2003): 635-653; no. 9 (2003): 764-778.

KRATOCHVIL, JIŘÍ. *Szomorú Isten.* [Sad God]. Budapest: Európa Kiadó, 2003.

KRAUSZ, TAMÁS. "A világrendszer és az önigazgatás a peresztrojka periódusában. A szocialista alternatíva bukásának történetéből: a belső és a nemzetközi komponens" (The World System and Self-Management in the Period of Perestroika. From the History of the Fall of the Socialist Alternative: the Internal and International Components). *Eszmélet* no. 33 (1997): 97-138.

KRAUSZ, TAMÁS. *Lenintől Putyinig* [From Lenin to Putin]. Budapest: La Ventana Kiadó, 2003.

LANIGNE, MARY. *The Economics of Transition from Social Economy to Market Economy.* (Macmillan Press Limited, 1995), pp. 260-264.

LÁNYI, ANDRÁS. "Hagyomány, szerep, azonosság" (Tradition, Role, Identity). *Arat a magyar.* (Harvesting Hungarians). A Szociálpolitikai Értesítő és a Fejlődéstanulmányok sorozat különszáma. Institute of Sociology of HAS, 1988.

LÁNYI, KAMILLA (2001): "Vázlat a globalizációnak nevezett jelenségkör értelmezéséről" (Sketches for the Interpretation of the Phenomena Called Globalisation). *Közgazdasági Szemle* no. 6 (2001): 498-519.

## Bibliography

LOSONCZI, ÁGNES. *Az életmód az időben, a tárgyakban és az értékekben* [Living in Time, Objects and Values]. Budapest: Gondolat, 1977.
———. *Ártó-védő társadalom.* [Damaging and Protecting Society]. Budapest: Közgazdasági és Jogi Könyvkiadó, 1989.
MARX, KARL. *Economic and Philosophic Manuscripts of 1844.* (Moscow: Progress Publishers, 1977), p.118.
MAULL, HANNS W. "Containing Entropy, Rebuilding the State: Challenges to International Order in Age of Globalization." *Internationale Politik und Gesellschaft. International Politics and Society* 2 (2002): 9–28.
MYRDAL, GUNNAR. *Value in Social Theory (A Selection of Essays on Methodology.)* Edited by Paul Streeten. London: Routledge and Kegan Paul, 1958. Reprinted in 1998 by Routledge, London.
NEE, VICTOR. "Social Inequality in Reforming State Socialism: Between Redistribution and Market in China." *American Sociological Review* 26, (1991): 267–281.
OFFE, CLAUS. *Capitalism by Democratic Design? Democratic Theory Facing the Triple Transition in East-Central Europe.* Paper Presented to IPSA Congress, Buenos Aires, July 1991.
OWEN, JOHN M. "Why American Hegemony is Here to Stay." In: *Internationale Politik und Gesellschaft. International Politics and Society* 1. (2003): 71–86.
PINE I., B. J. – VIKTOR, B. – BOYNTON, A. C. "Making Mass Customization Work." *Harvard Business Review* 71, no. 5 (1993): 108–117.
PITTI, ZOLTÁN. *Európai felzárkózás és/vagy versenyképességünk javítása.* (Catching up with Europe and/or Improving our Competitiveness.) Presentation at a meeting of the Hungarian Association of Economists, held on 19 November 2002.
POLÁNYI, KÁROLY. *Az archaikus társadalom és a gazdasági szemlélet. Tanulmányok.* [The Archaic Society and the Economic Aspect. Essays]. Budapest: Gondolat, 1976.
RAWLS, JOHN. *Az igazságosság elmélete* [A Theory of Justice]. Budapest: Osiris Kiadó, 1997. (Originally published by The Belknap Press of Harvard University Press, 1971.)
RESNICH, STEPHEN A. – WOLFF, RICHARD D. *Class Theory and History. Capitalism and Communism in the USSR.* New York and London: Routledge, 2002.
RIFKIN, JEREMY. *The Age of Access: The New Culture of Hypercapitalism, Where All of Life is a Paid-for Experience.* New York: Jeremy P. Tarcher/Putham, 2000.
SALGÓ, ISTVÁN. "Eladósodás és reformtörekvések" (Growing Debt and Reform Attempts). *Közgazdasági Szemle* no. 6 (1989): 160–172.
SÁRKÖZY, TAMÁS. "A tulajdonosi szervezet" (The Owners' Organization). *Gazdaság* no. 3 (1982): 25–39.
SCHAPIRO, LEONARD. *The Communist Party of the Soviet Union.* University Paperbacks. London: Methuen, 1966.
SCHWEITZER, IVÁN. *A vállalatnagyság* [Company Size]. Budapest: Közgazdasági és Jogi Könyvkiadó, 1982.
SIK, OTA. *Der dritte Weg. Die marxistisch-leninistische Theorie und die moderne Industriegesellchaft.* Hamburg: Hoffmann und Campe, 1972.
SIMON, JÁNOS (1994): "Politikai kultúra Magyarországon a 'Melankolikus forradalom' alatt és után" (Political Culture in Hungary During and After the 'Melancholic Revolution'). *Törésvonalak és értékválasztások.* (Fault Lines and Value Choices). Institute of Political Sciences, HAS, 1994. pp.171–190.
SPIRÓ, GYÖRGY. *Az ikszek* [The Xes]. Budapest: Szépirodalmi Könyvkiadó, 1981.
SZABÓ, KATALIN. "A munkaviszonyok fellazulása" (Loosening Working Conditions). *Információs Társadalom* vol. III, no. 1 (2003): 75–95.
SZALAI, ERZSÉBET. *Kiemelt vállalat – beruházás – érdek* [Privileged Company – Investment – Interest]. Budapest: Akadémiai Kiadó, 1981.

---. "Gazdasági és társadalmi válság. Azonosságok, eltérések, alternatívák" (Economic and Social Crisis. Identities, Differences, Alternatives). *Szereppróba*. (Rehearsing Roles). (Budapest: Századvég Kiadó, 1988), pp. 35-65.

---. "The New Elite." *Across Frontiers* 5, no 3 (Fall Winter 1989a): 25-32.

---. *Gazdasági mechanizmus, reformtörekvések és nagyvállalati érdekek* [Economic Mechanism, Reform Attempts and Big Company Interests]. Budapest: Közgazdasági és Jogi Könyvkiadó, 1989b.

---. "Útelágazás" (Cross-Roads). *Valóság* no. 8 (1990): 15-30. *Szereppróba*. (Rehearsing Roles). Budapest: Századvég Kiadó, 2000.

---. "A hatalom metamorfózisa?" (The Metamorphosis of Authority?) *Szereppróba* (Rehearsing Roles). (Századvég Kiadó, 1991): 166-198.

---. *A civil társadalomtól a politikai társadalom felé. Munkástanácsok, 1989-1993* [From Civil Society towards the Political Society. Workers' Councils, 1989-1993]. Budapest: T-Twins Kiadó, 1994.

---. "Notes from inside the Belly of the Whale. The Crisis of the Hungarian Cultural Elite and the Dilemmas of Intellectuals." *Post-Socialism and Globalization*. (1995) (Budapest, Új Mandátum Könyvkiadó, 1999), pp. 74-107.

---. *Az elitek átváltozása* [The Transformation of the Elites]. Budapest: Cserépfalvi Kiadó, 1996; Új Mandátum Kiadó, 1998.

---. *Gazdasági elit és társadalom a magyarországi újkapitalizmusban* [Economic Elite and Society in Hungarian New Capitalism]. Budapest: Aula Kiadó, 2001.

---. "The Economic Elite and Social Structure in the Hungarian New Capitalism." *Central European Political Science Review* vol 2, no 5 (Fall 2001): 115-150.

---. *Baloldal—új kihívások előtt* [The Left Facing New Challenges]. Budapest: Aula Kiadó, 2003a.

---. "Az én trónfosztása" (The Dethronement of the Ego). *Népszabadság* (22 March, 2003b): 19-20.

---. "Az újkapitalizmus intézményesülése—és válsága" (The Institutionalisation and Crisis of New Capitalism). *Népszabadság*, (25 October, 2003c): 17-18.

SZALAI, JÚLIA. "Társadalmi válság és reform-alternatívák" (Societal Crisis and Reform Alternatives.) *Arat a magyar*. (Harvesting Hungarians). A Szociálpolitikai Értesítő és a Fejlődés-tanulmányok sorozat különszáma. Institute of Sociology of HAS, 1988.

SZALAVETZ, ANDREA. "Hálózati szerveződés az 'új gazdaságban', a világgazdaság centrumában és azon kívül" (Network Organisation in the "New Economy" in the Core of the World Economy and Outside It). *Információs Társadalom* vol. III, no. 1. (2003).

SZAMUELY, LÁSZLÓ. *A közép- és kelet-európai átalakulás társadalmi költségei* [The Societal Cost of the Central and East European Transformation]. Budapest: KOPINT-DATORG, 1995.

SZELÉNYI, IVÁN – KOSTELLO, ERICH. "A piaci átmenet elmélete: Vita és szintézis" (The Theory of Market Transition. Debate and Synthesis). *Szociológiai Szemle* no. 2 (1996): 3-20.

SZELÉNYI, IVÁN – SZELÉNYI, BALÁZS. "Why Socialism Failed: Toward a Theory of System Breakdown—Cases of Disintegration of East-European State Socialism." *Theory and Society* 23 (1994): 211-231.

SZIGETI, PÉTER. "Államszocialista kísérletek—történelmi tanulságok" (State Socialist Experiments – Historical Lessons). *Eszmélet* no. 58 (2003): 37-73.

SZŰCS, JENŐ. *Vázlat Európa három történeti régiójáró* [A Sketch of the Three Historical Regions of Europe]. Budapest: Magvető Kiadó, 1983.

TAMÁS, GÁSPÁR MIKLÓS. "Új kelet-európai baloldal" (A New East European Left). *Eszmélet* no. 50 (2001): 30-53.

TARDOS, MÁRTON. "A szabályozott piac kialakításának feltételei" (Conditions of the Development of a Regulated Market). *Közgazdasági Szemle* no. 9 (1985): 86–97.
THUROW, LESTER C. *The Future of Capitalism, How Today's Economic Forces Shape Tomorrow's World.* Harmondsworth: Penguin Books, 1996.
TROTSKY, LEON. *The Revolution Betrayed.* New York: Pathfinder, 1972.
TROTZKI, L. D. "Der neue Kurs." *Die linke Opposition in der Sowjetunion 1923–1928.* Bd. I. Berlin, (1976): 250–388.
———. "Die Erklärung der fünfzehn: Vor dem Thermidor Revolution und Konterrevolution in Sowjetrussland." *Die linke Opposition in der Sowjetunion, 1923–1928.* Bd. V. West Berlin, (1977): 213–229.
VOSLENSKY, MICHAEL *Nomenklatura. Anatomy of the Soviet Ruling Class.* London-Sidney-Toronto: The Bodley Head, 1983.
VOSZKA, ÉVA. *Érdek és kölcsönös függőség* [Interest and Interdependence]. Budapest: Közgazdasági és Jogi Könyvkiadó, 1984.
WALLERSTEIN, EMMANUEL. "Globalization or the Age of Transition?" *International Sociology* 15, no. 2 (2000): 249–264.
WEBER, MAX. *Economy and Society.* (Berkeley–Los Angeles–London: University of California Press, 1978), pp. 926, 935.
WENT, ROBERT. *Globalizáció. Neoliberális feladatok, radikális válaszok* [Globalization: Neo-liberal Challenge, Radical Responses]. Budapest: Perfekt Gazdasági Tanácsadó, Oktató és Kiadó Rt., 2002.

DOWNTOWN CAMPUS LRC

J.S. Reynolds Community College
3 7219 00143 5521